TAKING SIDES

DAVID FIELD

Taking sides

INTER-VARSITY PRESS

INTER-VARSITY PRESS

*Universities and Colleges Christian Fellowship
39 Bedford Square, London WC1B 3EY*

© INTER-VARSITY PRESS, LONDON
First edition, February 1975

ISBN 0 85110 380 4

Printed in Great Britain by
Hunt Barnard Printing Ltd., Aylesbury, Bucks.

CONTENTS

PREFACE

Day by day, the mass media churn out a steady stream of conflicting moral pronouncements. Some confront us directly in news reports and documentaries. Others filter through more subtly in plays or review articles. They all face the Christian with a contemporary challenge which is both urgent and insistent. Can we, or can we not, apply the principles of our faith to the moral issues thrown up by everyday life in today's world?

In this book, I have tried to apply biblical principles to some of the knottier headline issues. The choice of themes is, of course, only a personal selection. The material included in each chapter has had to be selective too, but I hope the suggestions for further reading will help those who are interested to delve more deeply; and I trust that the questions for discussion will earth the debate in the kind of real-life situations readers face personally. The Bible will not allow us to ignore the people behind the problems. Nor will it condone so-called 'Christian' decisions which are made without reference to the main-line principles of God's revelation.

Most of these chapters first saw the light of day in a series of lectures given to the School of Christian Studies sponsored by St Helen's, Bishopsgate, and All Souls', Langham Place, at the City University, London. I am deeply grateful for the stimulus those occasions provided. My special thanks go also to the Rev. Stephen Palmer for his searching criticisms of the draft manuscript.

I shall always be glad to answer queries readers may have about anything I have written in this book.

Oak Hill College,
Southgate, London, N14 4PS

1 WHAT DOES THE BIBLE SAY?

This is a book which begins where others end. Rather like a rail commuter at a main-line terminus, its point of departure is one that others would treat as their destination.

It is based on two frankly Christian convictions about morality. The first is that God's character and God's will provide the only proper standard by which man can measure his ideas about goodness and rightness. And the second, closely linked, is that those who sincerely want to discover God's will about any specific moral issue must begin their search in the Bible. In other words, good qualities are those we see reflected in *God's character*; the right moral decision in any situation is the one that squares with *God's will*; and it is the *Bible* which supplies us with a unique source of information about both. That is the starting-place. Or, to change the metaphor, this is the foundation on which everything else rests.

Stated so briefly, these foundation principles cry out for a detailed explanation and – some would say – for a careful defence too. Books have been written with that end in view.[1] But they finish where this begins. Such basic studies are obviously vital, but they may bypass some of the larger difficulties ordinary people meet in bringing Christian principles to bear on the complex issues of modern life. It is all very well to establish the fundamental principle that doing the right thing means doing God's will, but it is not always so easy to

[1] This has been my aim in *Free to do Right* (IVP, 1973).

discern what course of action God's will dictates in a given situation. The added assurance that we can discover what God wills by reading the Bible may not turn out to be of very much practical help either. Hours of Bible reading will not automatically dispel the fog that shrouds some moral issues on which the Scriptures seem to have no clear directives.

The size of the problem

Broadly speaking, there are three kinds of situation in which the Christian may find it hard to come to right moral decisions, if he relies solely on the Bible for guidance.

The first and most obvious difficulty concerns those pressing contemporary moral issues on which *the Bible has nothing directly to say*. Writing in 1964, when he was Industrial Adviser to the Ministry of Economic Affairs, Sir Frederick Catherwood condemned those who 'preach as if God's Word is not relevant to men's relations to their fellows, that is to society as we find it'. But he goes on to confess in the same passage, 'Certainly it is no part of our case that there is a different verse from the Bible to solve every different moral problem in a highly complex industrial society'.[2] On some important issues the Bible appears to be silent. When the rights and wrongs of persuasive picketing or nuclear warfare (or a host of other topics which regularly make the headlines) are debated in the student union, the Christian may find himself stranded if he is asked to make a moral judgment on biblical grounds. So much of the media's vocabulary is absent from the pages of Scripture. In a book written centuries before the industrial revolution, how could it possibly be otherwise?

Then, secondly, there are those issues on which *the Bible's*

[2] H. F. R. Catherwood, *The Christian in Industrial Society* (IVP, 1964), p. xiii.

advice sounds embarrassingly outdated. A couple planning to get married, for example, might turn to Scripture for advice on family planning. If they leafed through Genesis they would find, not many pages after God's encouragement to Adam and Eve to 'be fruitful and multiply' (Gn. 1: 28), the parting message Rebekah's family gave her before she left home to become Isaac's bride: 'They blessed Rebekah, and said to her, "Our sister, be the mother of thousands of ten thousands" ' (Gn. 24: 60). If this is the biblical equivalent of a telegram saying 'God bless you on your wedding day', it does seem a little irresponsible to perpetuate such warm approval for multiple childbearing at a time when a population explosion is threatening the world's food supplies.

There are, moreover, times when *the Bible seems to give conflicting advice.* To take a commonplace example, honesty and politeness are two principles which Scripture endorses. Most of the time we can observe both, with no suspicion of any clash. But, as we all know, an occasion may arise when telling the strict truth would be most *im*polite! At a more serious level, many doctors are facing similar problems in their surgeries. When an unmarried girl asks her GP to prescribe a contraceptive, should he do so to limit the risks of an unwanted baby, or should he refuse her request to defend the principle of 'no sex outside marriage'? He might defend either decision on biblical grounds. The fact that the Bible can be made to speak with two voices leads the cynic to scorn all attempts to rely on Scripture for moral guidance. 'To a lawyer, theological discussion of the fundamentalist type makes fascinating reading', writes Professor Glanville Williams (tongue in cheek?). 'Fortunately there is always sufficient doubt and contradiction in the sacred texts to enable a commonsense result to be reached if the interpreter is willing to do so.'[3] And an anonymous clergyman writing for the Abortion Law Reform Association comes to much the same conclusion. 'I have always considered it futile to quote

[3] G. L. Williams, *The Sanctity of Life and the Criminal Law* (Faber, 1958).

texts from the Bible in support of an argument', he confesses, 'since precisely opposite texts can usually be found, if you know where to look for them.'[4]

Such a low view of the unity of Scripture would be hard to defend, but those who look to the Bible for clear-cut solutions to every moral problem that presents itself may – at any rate sometimes – find themselves disappointed. Life has many grey areas of moral decision-making. As Kenneth Greet aptly puts it, 'The man who sees everything in black and white is morally colour-blind'.[5]

False trails

In looking for reliable guide-lines, the Christian must beware of two attractive but misleading 'solutions'.

On one side, *the legalist* beckons. His simple way out of any moral dilemma is to make a rule to cover it. The commandments of the Bible are broken down into a vast network of moral by-laws, detailed enough to cover every conceivable set of circumstances, so that all the conscientious law-observer has to do is to classify his problem accurately and read off the answer in the rule-book. For the legalist, the process of making moral decisions is as simple and straightforward as that.

In New Testament days, the best-known exponents of the rule-book approach to morality were, of course, the scribes and Pharisees. With the praiseworthy aim of providing made-to-measure decisions for moral dilemmas of all shapes and sizes, they stitched rule upon regulation to cover any set of circumstances that might arise in ordinary daily life. Ingenuity and vivid imagination were both harnessed in a gigantic attempt to eliminate all moral doubts. In any clash

[4] Quoted by R. F. R. Gardner, *Abortion: The Personal Dilemma* (Paternoster, 1972), p. 113.
[5] K. G. Greet, *The Art of Moral Judgement* (Epworth, 1970), p. 88.

of responsibilities, the disciple (perhaps with the help of his ecclesiastical solicitor) could expect to find a ready-made solution somewhere in the pages of his rule-book.

Jesus' outspoken condemnation of the Pharisees' casuistry is enough to make any Christian ultra-cautious before setting out on the legalist's path to moral solutions. At its best, the rule-book approach is inadequate. No-one really needs to be told that wooden obedience to a long list of rules and regulations is a very poor substitute for positive moral living which springs from heartfelt conviction. Rules may be useful for restraining wrongdoing, but they are relatively useless for inspiring acts of outgoing love. As Lord Devlin put it, the law can provide floors for morality, but no ceilings.[6]

Jesus' many confrontations with the Pharisees show how easily legalism at its worst can turn basic moral values upside down. The Ten Commandments, for example, made it clear that a son should always respect and provide for his parents. At the same time the rest of the Bible teaches just as clearly that everything a man owns belongs as of right to God. The Pharisees attempted to reconcile these two principles by inventing a by-law which, in effect, allowed any unscrupulous individual to deny his ageing mother and father material help by declaring his property 'Corban' or 'God-dedicated'. In other words, the claims of family need could be set aside quietly under a pretext of piety. Jesus' comment is blunt and scathing: 'You make an excellent job of completely nullifying the commandment of God in order to observe your own tradition' (Mk. 7: 9). Slavery to the rule-book had made these leaders of religion 'good men in the worst sense of the word', as Mark Twain would have put it.

Then competing with the legalist for our attention is *the situationist*. To him, the rule-book route to successful moral living is absolutely anathema. As popularized by John Robinson in Britain and by Joseph Fletcher in America, the theory of situation ethics places exclusive emphasis on love. 'The ruling norm of Christian decision', writes Fletcher, 'is

[6] P. Devlin, *The Enforcement of Morals* (OUP, 1965), p. 23.

LOVE; nothing else.'[7] For the situationist, therefore, moral rules and regulations can play a helpful advisory role, but they are 'love's servants and subordinates, to be quickly kicked out of the house if they forget their place and try to take over'.[8] Love must be given full rein, even if it leads (on rare occasions) to acts of lying, stealing, extra-marital sex, or even murder.

Situationists like Fletcher and Robinson see Jesus as their supreme champion. It was Jesus, they point out, who led the way in putting people before principles, showing far more concern for a law-breaker like the woman taken in adultery than for the commandment she had broken (Jn. 7: 53 ff.). It was he who rebuked the legalistic approach to forgiveness Peter displayed when he asked how many times the rules obliged him to pardon an enemy (Mt. 18: 21 f.). And, of course, it was Jesus who telescoped all the rules and regulations of the Old Testament into the twin Christian love-obligations: 'You shall love the Lord your God with all your heart, and with all your soul, and with all your mind, and with all your strength . . . You shall love your neighbour as yourself' (Mk. 12: 30 f.).

As an escape from legalism, situation ethics is warmly attractive. But as an exposition of New Testament teaching it is woefully inadequate. A cursory reading of the Gospels reveals a Jesus who did not simply replace moral rules with the criterion of love. On some occasions he rated man's obligation to the Old Testament's moral law very highly indeed (e.g. Mt. 5: 17 ff.). He made it clear, too, that he required unswerving obedience to his own moral teaching (Mt. 7: 24 ff.). And, apparently without a trace of embarrassment, he described the perfect love-relationship he enjoyed with his Father in terms of his own full obedience to God's commandments (Jn. 15: 10).

It does not need much human insight to see exactly why, with the best will in the world, ordinary people need the

[7] J. Fletcher, *Situation Ethics* (SCM, 1966), p. 69.
[8] J. Fletcher, *op. cit.*, p. 78.

demands of love spelt out for them in very specific terms. To tell anyone to 'love and do what you like' is to put him at enormous risk, morally speaking. In *Honest to God*, John Robinson argues that 'love alone, because, as it were, it has a built-in moral compass, enabling it to "home" intuitively upon the deepest need of the other, can allow itself to be directed completely by the situation'.[9] Unfortunately, human nature proves otherwise. Self-deception finds ingenious ways of jamming the delicate homing devices of love's moral compass. Everyone is prone to rationalize his own weaknesses and to make exceptions in his own favour. It is all too easy, even for the morally sensitive, to convince oneself that a particular course of action is loving when in fact the motives are very mixed indeed. Few things are beyond the powers of human ingenuity to justify under the umbrella heading of 'love'.

The legalist and the situationist, then, lead us along false trails. The one strait-jackets moral living by filling the gaps in God's law with volumes of man-made by-laws. The other sits too loosely to the example and teaching of Jesus. The way ahead cannot lie through either expanding or compressing the Bible's moral directives. Somehow the Christian must find a middle course which follows Jesus' respect for the important role of law, while still allowing the individual flexibility to make his own moral decisions in the light of biblical teaching.

Guide-lines

There are five guiding principles which point the way towards a right use of Scripture in approaching contemporary moral issues.

1. Examine the context
The Bible is not a textbook bulging with abstract ethical theories. All its doctrine is grounded in real-life situations,

[9] J. A. T. Robinson, *Honest to God* (SCM, 1963), p. 115.

and to discover the relevance of any particular piece of moral teaching the very first step is to examine the context in which it appears. This will often act as a safeguard against drawing false conclusions. Many advocates of the monastic life, for example, have drawn their justification for taking vows of poverty from Jesus' encounter with the rich young ruler (Mk. 10: 17 ff.). What some have overlooked, however, is the fact that Jesus was not here intending to set up a standard of Christian living to which all top-class disciples should aspire. The context makes it plain that his aim was to make one self-centred man see that discipleship costs full commitment. There may still be individuals for whom the words 'sell what you have' strike home with the full literal force of a command from God, but the setting of this particular interview forbids us to conclude that if God's will were perfectly done, *all* Christians would be penniless.

The Old Testament's approval of large families also begins to make sense once it is read in context. The times were such that it was to the socio-economic advantage of all to have plenty of children. To transfer this teaching into the very different living conditions of today's world would clearly be a mistake. God's command was to replenish the earth, not to exhaust its resources by overcrowding.

A careful examination of biblical contexts, then, will prevent some of the more grotesque misapplications of isolated proof texts which tend to bring all Bible-based morality into disrepute. It will also give the Christian extra confidence as he applies the teaching of Scripture correctly to the modern issues on which his opinions are sought. Sometimes, for example, it is pointed out that the Bible's stern denunciations of extra-marital sex were directed to people who lived in an age before the vulcanization of rubber. At a time when VD could not be controlled, the argument goes, and when contraception was very much a hit-and-miss affair, it was clearly right to deter people from having sexual intercourse outside marriage. Nowadays, happily, antibiotics and the pill have revolutionized the sex scene. Viewed in context, therefore, these biblical warnings can safely be tucked away on some respectable shelf in a museum of biblical antiquities.

This sounds plausible enough, until the *theological* setting of the Bible's sex teaching is examined. Then it very quickly becomes plain that the *historical* context is only marginally relevant at this point. The moral case the Bible presents against extra-marital sex does not rest on the prevention of unwanted pregnancies and disease at all, but on the damage such behaviour causes to the human personality.[1] The relevance of these biblical vetoes, therefore, (which, of course, make up only one small part of the Bible's very positive approach to sexual behaviour) is unaffected by advances in VD treatment and contraceptive expertise. They rest on far deeper foundations – the nature of man as God created him and intends him to be.

So many of the Bible's moral demands, whatever their setting in time and place, must be seen in their broader theological context which often defies the eroding effects of historical change. Pride, jealousy, love, kindness and all the other basic moral categories in which Scripture deals are as lasting as human nature itself. Amos' cheating tradesmen have been in their graves for centuries, but, as we know, their spirit lives on today in the High Streets of any modern capital city. The complacency this Old Testament prophet condemned in his acquisitive society more than 700 years before Christ is still matched by the attitude of the modern consumer who wakes up to the world shortage of fossil fuels only when petrol is rationed at *his* garage. It would clearly be wrong to trap this kind of teaching too tightly in its narrower historical setting. Archbishop Donald Coggan was not being unfaithful to the broader context of Amos' prophecy when he was reported in a church newspaper as saying, 'I think Amos might say to us . . . "You have polluted my world, therefore shall your supplies dry up and your lungs choke . . . You have made a valley into a dust bowl,

[1] *E.g.* 1 Corinthians 6:18, where 'body' has more than a physical significance.

therefore I will visit you with agricultural chaos . . . You have burned up my oil supplies with which I have enriched my world, therefore will I raise up a Sheik Yamani, who will be my weapon of judgment against you".[2]

2. Distinguish the 'weightier matters'

According to Jesus, one of the Pharisees' worst faults was that they were so preoccupied with the small print of the moral law that they lost track of its main headings. They tithed their herb gardens meticulously, but ignored 'the weightier matters of the law, justice and mercy and faith' (Mt. 23: 23). Small things filled their minds so completely that the really big things escaped their notice altogether.

By this Jesus did not mean that it was wrong to pay attention to detail ('these you ought to have done'), but his words imply that moral obligations can be graded. In some situations this may mean that matters of lesser importance have to be bypassed (at least temporarily) in favour of greater duties. During the run-up to a general election, for example, the Christian is unlikely to find that any one manifesto contains all the policies he would like to see, but in making his choice he will want to weigh the relative importance of the various issues the political parties present to him. In particular, he will be on the look-out for the main-line themes of biblical social concern (such as protection for the weak and defenceless, justice for the victimized and reverence for human life), and he will make up his mind how to vote in the light of the answers he gets.

This 'league table' approach may leave the Christian feeling desperately uneasy, but the need to put moral obligations in some order of priority was felt just as keenly in New Testament times as it is in our own. The Council of Jerusalem in Acts 15, for example, was faced with a situation in which at least three important principles were at stake. Some argued strongly that Gentile converts should observe Jewish conventions so as to show the link between the

[2] *Church of England Newspaper*, 25 January 1974.

Christian church and God's people of Old Testament times. Others countered by pointing out that it would be quite wrong to enmesh Gentile Christians in the soul-sapping demands of Jewish legalism. The Council, in its wisdom, decided that both sides should yield ground in favour of a third principle, *which in this case must take precedence* – that of Christian unity. Gentiles were to be freed from any obligation to the ceremonial law, but in order to show their solidarity with their more scrupulous Jewish brethren they should eat their food *kosher*.

3. Choose the lesser evil

The Bible encourages the Christian to go for the big things in making moral decisions. But sometimes situations arise in which the choice seems to lie between two evils, rather than between greater and lesser goods. It is a case of staying in the frying-pan or jumping into the fire. A gynaecologist operating to terminate a pregnancy, for example, faces this kind of moral dilemma. If he carries through with the operation, he will destroy the life of a foetus; if he refuses, he may well put the woman's life at risk. Whichever choice he makes, some bad consequence is unavoidable.

The Bible is a realistic book, and it does not pretend that such mind-twisting problems need never occur in a world saturated with sin. Its practical advice is that the Christian, when faced with this kind of decision, should always choose the least evil of the options open to him. The question of divorce provides a biblical illustration of this principle at work. The Old Testament is quite explicit about God's marriage standards: 'Therefore a man leaves his father and his mother and cleaves to his wife, and they become one flesh' (Gn. 2: 24). In the New Testament we find Jesus quoting these words from Genesis to uphold the principle of the permanence of marriage. But he also admitted, when challenged, that Moses had allowed divorce, to make room for the consequences of man's 'hardness of heart'. And he himself went on to make one significant exception to his general

19

ban on divorce and remarriage: 'except for unchastity' (Mt. 19: 3 ff.). So the Bible does recognize that in some situations God's ideal marriage standards simply cannot be reached. Sometimes a marriage relationship may be so ruined that separation or divorce becomes the lesser evil. This does not mean that God's standards change. He still hates divorce (Mal. 2: 16). But, although still evil, occasions may arise when divorce is not quite so bad as any available alternative.

Any Christian is naturally reluctant to make these lesser-evil choices. They smell strongly of compromise, and some will certainly brand them as such. Complete withdrawal, which is sometimes the only alternative, may look a far more attractive option. 'Sometimes', confesses one Christian gynaecologist, 'we feel like withdrawing from the controversy, just opting out . . . and refusing to see patients requesting abortion. But', she goes on, 'would this be right? Surely it is essential for Christians to face up to their problems, not to escape from them.'[3] Opting out is, in fact, a more apparent than real alternative to involvement. As Jesus taught, especially in the parable of the Good Samaritan, to do *nothing* in a situation that calls for action is actually to do *something*. Either way, there is no escape from responsibility.

4 Weigh the interests of others

If the last few paragraphs have built up a picture of the Christian as a person who strides confidently through life's great problems, flipping out a pocket calculator from time to time to make moral decisions between greater goods and lesser evils with cold mathematical precision, the image is clearly a false one. Rex Gardner puts his finger on the missing factor when he tells, against himself, the story of a young girl who was referred to him for an abortion. She was only sixteen, and she had already had one abortion the previous year. After making sure she was pregnant and healthy, Gardner was blunt and brief in his rejection of her request

[3] Miss E. Sibthorpe, quoted by R. F. R. Gardner, *Abortion: The Personal Dilemma*, p. 137.

for termination. 'Recounting that case to a colleague, shortly after,' he writes, 'it suddenly struck me to wonder if that is the manner in which the Lord Jesus would have talked to the girl, had He been the consulting gynaecologist? The next morning my ordinary routine Bible reading reached the passage where Christ says: "Be compassionate as your Father is compassionate. Pass no judgment and you will not be judged. Do not condemn and you will not be condemned. Acquit and you will be acquitted." That was God's word to me about the case. I have never doubted that I was right in rejecting her request; I was wrong in my manner of doing so.'[4]

Right at the centre of Jesus' ethical teaching is love, and love focuses on people. The situationists are absolutely right in drawing our attention to the vital importance of the personal factor in making moral choices. Moral cases involve broken relationships; they involve men and women who have been hurt, disillusioned or misled. Over and above clinical diagnoses and calculated solutions, they need compassionate understanding and practical help.

Concern for other people will always determine the way a moral decision is put across. It may also radically change the choice that is made. In his letter to the church at Rome, for example, Paul points out that some things which in themselves are morally legitimate become bad when they result in harm to others. Certainly the interests of others must play a weighty role in Christian decision-making, even if love means that we do not always give way to a specific request (e.g. giving the price of a drink to an alcoholic). The worker who agrees to take strike action without any thought for those who will suffer as the result of his action, and the penologist who carefully calculates the retributive justice and social effect of a punishment without taking into account the needs of the offender (and the victim), are both making moral decisions which, on Christian grounds, are deficient in a vital respect. They have lost sight of the people behind the cases – and that is something Jesus never did.

[4] R. F. R. Gardner, *op. cit.*, p. 129.

5. Listen to the voice of conscience

Conscience is not an infallible guide. It may, in the Bible's vivid terminology, be anaesthetized (literally, 'seared', 1 Tim. 4: 2) by habitual wrongdoing, so that it fails to give strong warning signals when it should. The first time a man tells a lie, he will probably go very red in the face because his conscience pricks him. But if he becomes practised in lying, after a few years he will be able to look his victims straight in the eye while telling the most enormous untruths. The voice of conscience can be silenced. Curiously, too, conscience may sometimes give false guidance through being *over*-sensitive. The strict teetotaller who eventually comes to the conclusion that there is nothing wrong for him in the occasional drink will almost certainly suffer pangs of conscience when he first puts his new conviction into practice. If he has reached his decision on Christian grounds (convinced, perhaps, that the Bible puts no ban on alcohol), he may find encouragement in the New Testament's assurance that 'God is greater than our conscience' (1 Jn. 3: 20, NEB).

The voice of conscience, then, is not always the voice of God. But with consistent growth in the Christian life it can become, increasingly, the vehicle by which God makes his will known. As well as being anaesthetized by sin, conscience can be educated through closer acquaintance with the Bible's teaching until, in Spurgeon's words, 'it should shiver whenever the ghost of a sin goes by'. In practical terms, this will mean that in cases of genuine doubt the Christian will always avoid a course of action which his conscience vetoes. As paul puts it, 'if a man considers a particular thing impure, then to him it is impure' (Rom. 14: 14, NEB).

Nor is the guidance of conscience merely negative. The really distinctive mark of a Christian, according to the Bible, is that the Spirit of God lives in him (Rom. 8: 9 ff.). And the Holy Spirit is no sleeping partner. He is the believer's spiritual and moral dynamic. *'God is at work in you,'* writes Paul, 'both to will and to work for his good pleasure' (Phil.

2: 13). Through the Spirit's dynamism, the Christian becomes increasingly sensitive to the things which please God, and increasingly capable of acting according to his will. Conscience, after all, is only the umbrella title we put over the whole area of our moral sensitivity. It is only to be expected that as our moral outlook becomes aligned more and more closely to the will of God, the guidance of conscience will become more and more reliable.

Guide-lines are not rules. On many occasions, the Bible's few basic rules for moral living will be quite enough to sort out right from wrong. But in other more complex situations (like most of those with which this book deals), decisions will not come so easily. The guide-lines will help to clarify the main issues. They will not necessarily lead to quick and easy solutions – or even to the same solutions. Often, because moral cases involve people, the choices may be particularly hard to make. But armed with an open Bible, and confident that the Holy Spirit will guide the decisions of those whose minds are open to his direction, the Christian has all the resources he needs to make right moral judgments. In the words of the Letter to the Hebrews, those who feed on the 'solid food' of God's Word 'have their faculties trained by practice to distinguish good from evil' (Heb. 5: 14).

2 MAN AND NATURE

A man who set out systematically to destroy his own home might be persuaded to see a psychiatrist. If he tried to break up other people's homes too, he would have to be restrained by the law. However tolerant society might become, it would be hard to foresee a state of affairs in which an individual could be allowed to ruin other people's lives, as well as his own, with impunity.

This is the message the ecological prophets have been trying to get across to us for a long time now. Spell man with a capital 'M', they say, and the parallel with the broken home becomes overwhelmingly obvious. The planet which has been mankind's home for centuries is now threatened by careless, criminal exploitation at the hands of its present occupants. By unthinking use of natural resources, modern man is making a home that will not be fit for his children to live in, a world in which his grandchildren may find it hard to survive. And together with his own posterity, he seems intent on dragging the rest of creation into disaster with him. Opinions may differ as to whether it is a doctor we need, or a policeman, but urgent action of some kind is obviously necessary if the family home is to remain inhabitable.

The size of the problem

The ecologists' warnings cannot be dismissed as mere alarmist talk, because there is plenty of evidence to back them up. At *ground level*, for example, it is sobering to realize that the famous fertile crescent of the Middle East, which used to support whole empires, has now become a strip of desert as a result of man's mismanagement. Naturalists tell us that the Sahara in West Africa is advancing at the rate of twenty miles a year, partly through climatic changes, but mainly because the sparse vegetation at its edges is being over-grazed. Much of the fault can no doubt be traced to man's ignorance rather than to his negligence, but the same excuse can hardly be advanced for the massive destruction of wood-land involved in getting a national newspaper into print. It has been calculated that just one Sunday edition of the *New York Times* gobbles up 150 acres of forest[1] – and replace-ment trees grow very slowly, despite all the efforts of Forestry Commissions.

Conservationists point out that it is not only future gene-rations of men who will feel the effects of this kind of devas-tation. When trees are chopped down and hedges removed to make way for mechanized cultivation and combine harvesting, wild-life suffers too. If birds and animals lose their habitats, they die as surely as if they eat poison, and the fact that nearly 300 kinds of mammals (and an even greater number of birds) are now on the endangered species list is something as morally wrong as lack of neighbour-love. Can man go on thumbing his nose at the rest of creation and remain blameless? The words of a pop song, 'Strange Days', vividly express the moral indignation many conservationists feel:

> 'What have they done to the earth,
> What have they done to our fair sister?
> Ravaged and plundered and ripped her and bit her,
> Stuck her with knives in the side of the dawn
> And tied her with fences and dragged her down.'

Water pollution is another serious problem that finds its way into the headlines more and more frequently. Lakes and

[1] G. Schwab, *Dance with the Devil* (Bles, 1963), p. 117.

seas are used as dumping-grounds for man's garbage, and some of the more refined rubbish comes home in a disconcerting way (tinned tuna fish with a high mercury content, as well as oil slicks on the holiday beaches). Then there are the phosphates from fertilizers and detergents that find their way into rivers and promote the excessive growth of algae, which, in turn, eventually choke the waterways. The oxygen content of some rivers and lakes has dropped to such an alarming level as a result of agricultural and industrial pollution that they can no longer cope with the constant flow of sewage and other waste matter that is remorselessly pumped into them. Within living memory people used to swim and fish in Lake Erie for pleasure. Anyone who accidentally falls into that lake's stinking water nowadays is strongly advised to have a tetanus injection.

Most obviously of all, *pollution affects the air* we breathe. Car exhaust fumes discharge lead into the atmosphere in quantities some experts regard as a health hazard, while in heavily industrialized areas factory chimneys pump out 1,000 tons of grit per square mile each year, or so it has been estimated. In Tokyo, oxygen-vending slot-machines have been installed for public use, so commuters waiting for their trains can choose whether to buy a bar of chocolate or a breath of fresh air for the journey. And one committee of scientists has even come up with the disturbing hypothesis that the combustion products of aircraft engines may eventually accumulate in the upper atmosphere and affect the earth's climate.

The picture, of course, is not an altogether gloomy one. In recent years, conditions have improved vastly in many places, thanks mainly to the influence of pressure groups on local government. London, for example, now enjoys 50 per cent more winter sunshine than it did in 1956, the year the first Clean Air Act was passed, and atmospheric pollution dropped so dramatically in Manchester as a result of Clean Air legislation that the municipal authorities considered it worth while to wash the Town Hall. Nevertheless, while the

Thames in Central London (after being virtually fishless for a century) yielded specimens of forty different kinds of fish in 1968, a court in Chelmsford, not very many miles away, could still let an industrial firm off with a token fine of £25 for discharging enough cyanide into the River Chelmer to kill 63,000 fish and cause the river to be taken temporarily out of the public water-supply system.[2]

What happens to the Thames or the Chelmer may be of immediate concern only to the handful of people who call the south-east corner of England their home, but world statesmen are agreed that the problems of conserving natural resources and coping with pollution are of the most far-reaching significance for the whole of mankind. Speaking in a UNO debate a few years ago, the United States representative said: 'I believe that environmental problems will appear, in the perspective of the years, as of incomparably greater importance to the human species than the many political dissensions to which we devote such a great part of our days and nights at the United Nations.'[3] And U Thant, then United Nations Secretary-General, supported him. 'There is arising a crisis of world-wide proportions,' he said, 'involving developing and developed countries alike – the crisis of the human environment . . . It is becoming apparent that, if current trends continue, the future of life on earth could be endangered.'[4]

The Bible and nature

If predictions like these are accurate, it is easy to understand why many of our contemporaries become extremely impatient and irritated when they see Christians spending so

[2] Lord Kennet, *Controlling our Environment* (Fabian Society, 1970), pp. 11, 19.
[3] James Wiggins, at a UNO plenary session on 3 December 1968.
[4] In the Introduction to *Problems of the Human Environment*, a Report to the 47th Session of UNO, May 1969.

much of their time and effort fighting such things as pornography and gambling, while the world they say God created and loves threatens to come crashing in ruins about their ears. It also adds point to the embarrassing question Schaeffer addresses to his readers in *Pollution and the Death of Man*. 'As a Christian', he asks, 'what relationship have you thought of and practised towards nature as your fellow-creature, over the last ten years?'[5] We preach about our relationship with God. We debate family relations, race relations, and industrial relations. But how much thought do we give, as Christians, to our relationship with the rest of creation?

There are sound historical reasons why a question of this kind is likely to catch the average Christian reader off his guard. From the earliest times there has been a persistent tradition in the church favouring a coolly indifferent attitude to nature. It takes only a little Bible study, however, to discover that such a careless approach to the world of creation owes far more to Gnostic dualism than it does to the doctrines of Scripture. Some early religious thinkers may have written off material things as irrelevant, and even hostile, to the spiritual life; but the Bible insists that God is as concerned with the welfare of his material creation as he is with the spiritual progress of the redeemed.

It is particularly impressive to see how, again and again, at the key points of the Bible's story, the destiny of man is closely bound up with that of his environment. At the time of the Fall, we are told that the consequences of Adam's disobedience affected not only his own future but even the ground he walked on: 'cursed is the ground because of you', said God (Gn. 3: 17). Then, after the Flood, we are shown the other side of the coin, as God's promise to Noah specifically takes in the rest of creation as well as mankind: 'the covenant which I make between me and you and every living creature that is with you' (Gn. 9: 12).

The same note is struck in Exodus. The Bible tells us that

[5] F. A. Schaeffer, *Pollution and the Death of Man* (Hodder, 1970), p. 56.

the blood of the Passover sacrifice availed not only for the people but for their animals (just as the Egyptian animals, as well as the people, suffered the death of the first-born – Ex. 11: 4–7); while, out in the desert, the Ten Commandments laid it down that the animals should have a share in the household's sabbath day's rest (Ex. 20: 10). And when, at last, the people of Israel were able to leave the desert and cross the Jordan, God gave them instructions for the agricultural care and conservation of the promised land, alongside laws designed for the welfare of men and women (Lv. 25).

The New Testament echoes the same theme. When Jesus wanted a suitable illustration to show how much God cares for the individual, he hit upon the analogy of a good shepherd hunting high and low for his lost animal. The main purpose of the illustration was, of course, to spotlight the love of God for *people*, but the fact that God's love could be described in terms of the relationship between a shepherd and his sheep tells us a great deal about the care man should have for *animals*. Any good herdsman, Jesus implied, values his animals highly enough to risk his life for them (unlike the man whose only interest in the job is his wage-packet at the end of the week – Jn. 10: 11, 12). He knows them well enough to call them individually by name (Jn. 10: 3), and he notices when just one out of a hundred goes missing (Mt. 18: 12).

We may notice in passing that to call someone by his name is a mark, in the Bible, of a very special relationship. Significantly, the Psalmist tells us that God extends this sign of his personal care to the whole of creation. Even inanimate matter finds a place under the umbrella of God's special concern as he 'determines the number of the stars' and 'gives to all of them their names' (Ps. 147: 4). And the way God brings the different animals to Adam to be named (Gn. 2: 19) shows that man is intended to share his Maker's care for the welfare of creation. Indifference to the suffering of a horse transported across the Channel, or to the fate of a dog dumped in a local park because it is no longer wanted, amounts to a denial of the God-given responsibility implicit in this naming ceremony.

In the light of this basic creation teaching, and Jesus' use of analogies from animal husbandry to illustrate God's compassionate love, some aspects of modern factory farming seem especially hard to justify. A girl who has sole charge of 26,000 hens, and whose only duties are to remove dead birds and transfer the eggs to a conveyor belt, can hardly be expected to show the individual care for living things that Jesus tacitly commended in his good shepherd illustration. Something like this was no doubt in the minds of the members of the government-sponsored Brambell Committee in 1965 when they pointed out that increased mechanization in hen husbandry demands even better and more skilled supervision than traditional methods. 'There is a real danger', their report adds, 'that long-scale intensive methods involving great numbers of animals, possibly in surroundings which are uncomfortable to man, can lead to a debasement in the stockman's attitude to the lives for which he has a responsibility.'

If Jesus' teaching mirrors the intense care God lavishes now on all created things, a remarkable passage in Paul's letter to the Romans sets out the important place creation will occupy after the cosmic upheaval of the last days. 'All creation', he writes, 'is waiting patiently and hopefully for that future day when God will glorify His children. For on that day thorns and thistles, sin, death, and decay that overcame the world against its will . . . will all disappear, and the world around us will share in the glorious freedom from sin which God's children enjoy.' Just as everything created has been contaminated by man's fall into sin, so the whole of creation will be transformed when, in God's plan, the moment for man's final redemption arrives. 'For we know', concludes Paul, 'that even the things of nature, like animals and plants, groan in sickness and death as they await this great event' (Rom. 8: 19–22, Kenneth Taylor, *Living Letters*; *cf*. Jas. 1: 18).

According to the Bible, then, man's environment is bound up with him in his final destiny. The same God who created everything at the beginning, and who maintains the balance of nature now by 'upholding the universe by his word of power' (Heb. 1: 3), will, one day, transform all things, as well as Christian people, in his redeeming power. Scripture militates strongly against a 'men only' view of creation. If, therefore, we shrug our shoulders at the suffering of animals and birds, the plight of trees or the spoiling of land – because, as Christians, we believe such things are beneath our concern – our ideas are clearly out of tune with the mind of God.

Creatures and managers

When we probe a little more deeply, we find that the Bible defines man's relationship with the rest of creation in two main ways:

1. As fellow-creature
It was Adam and Eve's proud desire to rise above their creatureliness and 'become as gods' (the serpent's words) that drew from the Lord God the stern reminder 'You are *dust,* and to dust you shall return' (Gn. 3: 19). The church-goer may not have very much in common with the pew on which he sits now, but in a century or so's time there may not be a great deal, physically, to distinguish them (unless, of course, the pew is made of plastic, in which case it may well outlast the sitter).

Creatureliness is a humbling concept. The realization that man is regularly outlived by such things as a yew tree and a tortoise is hardly conducive to human pride. Yet the fact that, when he faces nature, man is facing things which share his basic chemical make-up should at least awaken within him a brotherly respect for everything else that is created. Francis of Assisi's description of the birds as 'our brethren' may sound rather sentimental, but the biblical truth that lies behind his words is too important to be obscured by modern talk of 'natural assets' and 'world resources'. Our obligation to other created things goes far beyond the rate-payer's duty to return library books in a fit condition for the next borrower. The family ties of creation demand that all other creatures must be respected for their own sake, not merely for the benefit of the next consumer in the queue.

2. *As manager*

As a creature, man is on a level with the rest of creation. But that is only half the biblical story. The early chapters of Genesis certainly emphasize the hugeness of the gap which separates the Creator from everything that is created, including mankind, but they also clearly tell how God marked man off from everything else he made by creating him in his own image (Gn. 1:27). And the very first command God gave man and woman set them apart still further from the rest of creation: 'God blessed them, and God said to them, "Be fruitful and multiply, and fill the earth and subdue it; and have dominion over the fish of the sea and over the birds of the air and over every living thing that moves upon the earth" ' (Gn. 1: 28). By divine appointment, man was made *manager* of creation, and though he soon forfeited all rights to that office by his disobedience, we find the same command repeated by God after the Fall (Gn. 3. 23), and again after the Flood (Gn. 9: 1, 2).

Together with his creation in God's image, these orders from the Creator encourage man to probe the secrets of the universe and to harness its energy. Here is all the justification we need for modern scientific research and technological development. In so far as both are essentials for good management, man's vocation is not to leave nature scrupulously as he finds it, but to understand, develop and control its resources.

Creatureliness and dominion, then, are twin aspects of biblical teaching that must somehow hold together if our understanding of man's relationship with the rest of creation is to be complete. The Old Testament captures the blend perfectly in Psalm 8. Looking up at the night sky, the Psalmist is at first lost in amazement that God should be concerned about man's fate at all:

'When I look at thy heavens, the work of thy fingers,
    the moon and the stars which thou hast established;
what is man that thou art mindful of him,
    and the son of man that thou dost care for him?'

But then other facts of life come to mind, as he answers his own question.

'Yet thou hast made him little less than God,
    and dost crown him with glory and honour.
Thou hast given him dominion over the works of thy
      hands;
    thou hast put all things under his feet.'

Man, tiny piece of creation though he is, has been set in a position of awe-inspiring authority.

The poetry of the Psalm is vivid, but the balance is an extremely delicate one to maintain. As man walks his Creator's tightrope over a fallen world, there are many pressures which threaten to topple him to the one side or to the other. Or, to change the metaphor, *creatureliness* and *dominion* hold the two ends of a tug-of-war rope. While they are held in tension, all is well between man and his environment. But once either is pulled over the line, ecological disaster threatens.

Domination

This threat is worth investigating in more detail. First, if man loses a sense of creatureliness, his dominion over nature very quickly becomes harsh domination. The brotherly respect for God's creation, which Francis of Assisi spoke about and exemplified, is all too easily replaced by an arrogant disregard which many critics of the church confuse with

3

orthodox Christian doctrine. Ian McHarg, for example, referring to man's commission in Genesis to 'fill the earth and subdue it', writes: 'If you want to find one text of compounded horror which will guarantee that the relationship of man to nature can only be destruction, which will atrophy any creative skill, which will explain all of the destruction and all of the despoliation accomplished by western man these 2,000 years, then you do not have to look any further than this ghastly calamitous text.' Lynn White, professor of History at the University of California, is equally pointed. The contemporary environmental crisis, he claims, is all Christianity's fault, because the Bible's teaching that man is meant to exercise dominion over creation has encouraged men to treat nature in á destructive way. 'Our present science and our present technology', he concludes, 'are tinctured with orthodox Christian arrogance.'[8]

As a criticism of Christian doctrine, this kind of comment is most unfair. In its biblical context (which, as we have seen, lays a great deal of emphasis on human creatureliness), the dominion God tells man to exercise over nature is not at all the same thing as the domination Ian McHarg and Lynn White condemn. Nevertheless, as an exposure of some Christians' conduct, the criticism stands up. Perhaps the most notorious example in church history of a callous disregard for nature is provided by the so-called 'Black Stocking Calvinists' of Holland, who taught that maltreating animals is quite permissible on Christian grounds because only people have souls. But other examples could just as easily be cited. When the Bible's teaching on man's dominion over the rest of creation is not balanced by a recognition of his creatureliness, the result is a domineering attitude which only too often is both thoughtless and cruel. And whenever the church has been guilty of championing this lop-sided view of biblical doctrine, it has every reason to be thoroughly ashamed.

[8] L. White, 'The Historical Roots of our Ecologic Crisis' (a lecture, quoted by F. A. Schaeffer, *Pollution and the Death of Man*, p. 85).

Pantheism

Once the idea of creatureliness goes, good management becomes arrogant domination. But the final result is no better, from a Christian point of view, if the other end of the rope is pulled over the line. If the Bible's teaching about man's creatureliness is stressed to a point where the idea of his managing creation is entirely lost, the outcome is not Christianity at all, but pantheism. According to the pantheist's scale of values, a human being is not worth any more than a tree or a hippopotamus. He therefore denies man's right to exercise any dominion over nature at all.

The pantheistic view of life, popularized by Lennon and the hippies, has for some time now been advocated as the only correct religious approach to man's ecological dilemma. In his novel *Island*, for example, Aldous Huxley forecasts a future in which a child's first school-lessons will be in ecology, not the 'three Rs'. In the reformed educational system he foresees, religious instruction will be based on pantheistic eastern religions, not Christianity, because 'elementary ecology leads straight to elementary Buddhism'.[7] Some prominent churchmen have also leaned hard in this direction. Hugh Montefiore, Anglican Bishop of Kingston, whose books on environmental issues have deservedly attracted a good deal of attention, confesses that 'the history of Christians' exploitation of nature makes a sorry story compared with Jain and Buddhist attitudes towards our fellow-creatures on this earth'.[8] His critics would claim that Albert Schweitzer's insistence on 'reverence for life' also came very close to pantheism.[9] It is rumoured that Schweitzer would not even allow a fly to be swatted in his operating theatre at Lambaréné, because he refused to recognize any distinction between so-called higher and lower forms of life.

[7] A. Huxley, *Island* (Penguin, 1970), p. 220.
[8] H. Montefiore, *Can Man Survive?* (Fontana, 1970), p. 46.
[9] *Cf.* A. Schweitzer, *The Teaching of Reverence for Life* (Peter Owen, 1965), p. 47; F. A. Schaeffer, *Pollution and the Death of Man*, pp. 20, 26, 36.

The attraction of pantheism lies in the dignity it gives to all non-human creation. Its failing, from a biblical viewpoint, is that it denies to man the managing role which God has assigned to him. To allow rats to spread disease, and cows to eat the food people desperately need, may be praiseworthy as an attempt to elevate the status of animals, but it lowers the status of man to a level Christian teaching cannot tolerate. Jesus stated quite bluntly that the value of an animal cannot compare with the value of a man (Mt. 12: 12). Though God does not overlook a single sparrow, 'you are of more value many sparows', he taught his disciples (Lk. 12: 7).

It is easy to talk glibly about 'co-operating with nature', but the realities of life leave little room for sentiment. The purple-headed mountain, which sounds so attractive in the children's hymn, may in some latitudes erupt and blot out the homes and livelihoods of thousands who live on its slopes. Thor Heyerdahl, the Norwegian explorer, once set out to find his own utopia on an 'unspoilt' Pacific island, only to discover that disease and cruelty had arrived long before he did. Later he wrote sadly. 'There is no Paradise to be found on earth today. There are people living in great cities who are far happier than the majority of those in the South Seas. Happiness comes from within, we realise that now . . . '[1]

Because it is a realistic book, the Bible does not disguise the fact that man will always find nature reluctant to accept his attempts to manage it. Rather like a prison governor, he must always expect to meet resistance from some quarters, however good his intentions, and this will make his task distasteful as well as difficult. Since the time of the Fall, when relationships of every kind were spoilt, man's environment has not been friendly to him. Inevitably, therefore, management will sometimes take on the appearance of oppression, but as we have seen, God did not revoke his instructions to Adam after the Fall. Man is not intended to maintain an uneasy *status quo* in nature, but to manage it.

[1] Quoted by R. J. Berry, *Ecology and Ethics* (IVP, 1972), p. 27.

Without any sense of shame, he can kill a rat, eliminate a virus or change the course of a river. The fact that he too is a created being brands harshness and cruelty as *mis-management*, but the dominion God has called him to exercise over his fellow-creation is far-reaching.

Stewardship

A balance, then, must be struck between man's nature as *creature* and his role as *manager*; and *stewardship* is the biblical category into which they both fit.

Any steward has two major responsibilities. The first is to treat his resources with respect and restraint. Because they are not his to squander, the goods in his care must not be wasted. As far as man's dominion over nature is concerned, the Bible makes it quite clear that in giving him control of creation, God has not relinquished over-all sovereignty. The earth is still the Lord's (Ps. 24: 1). He remains 'head over all' (1 Ch. 29: 11). Man's possession is therefore leasehold not freehold, which means that nothing he finds in God's world is expendable. 'Even if tigers have to be confined to game parks', a recent conference of Christian research scientists concluded, 'and yellow fever mosquitoes extirpated from areas where they might carry yellow fever, we should hope to preserve the species if possible.'[2]

A steward must not waste his goods, but his responsibilities do not end with conservation. In Jesus' parable of the talents, the man who carefully conserved what he had been given, but did not make any use of it, was condemned, not praised (Mt. 25: 26, 27). As God's steward of creation, man is called to put its resources to wise use; and the 'faithful and wise steward', according to Jesus, is the one who, when entrusted with the care of the household, 'gives them their portion of food at the proper time' (Lk. 12: 42). In the

[2] From a report of discussions at the Research Scientists' Christian Fellowship conference, 1972 (in *Christian Graduate*, June 1973, p. 58).

world, God has given man the key to his well-stocked larder; and man's corresponding duty is not to hoard all the goods, but to see to their fair and sensible distribution.

In the light of these twin responsibilities, some of the ethical issues become a little clearer. If a tree is needed to build a house, for example, it should be cut down and its wood used. That is good stewardship. But if it stands in the path of a new road which could just as easily be slightly re-routed to avoid it, the contractors should be instructed to bulldoze round it, even at a little extra expense – because trees matter. Unlike the Jain, who must never kill an insect, the Christian is at liberty to kill the fly he finds in the family larder, but a steward's respect for the Master's creation will stop him stamping on an ant he meets during a walk through the woods. A sacred cow may be slaughtered for food and a fox shot to protect the chickens, but to kill animals, birds or fish just for pleasure is to squander the Master's resources (as well as displaying an arrogance towards man's fellow-creatures which goes right against the spirit of Scripture).

By no means all problems, of course, are capable of simple solutions once the standards of stewardship are applied. Vivisection is one of the more thorny issues which leave many Christians in two minds. If the performing of experiments on living animals is not absolutely essential to human welfare, the question resolves itself, but on this score the evidence conflicts. While the Medical Research Council believes that 'animal experimentation is likely to be necessary for the foreseeable future',[3] others disagree. Professor S. T. Aygun of Ankara University, for example, argues that 'tissue and cell culture methods are in general superior to animal experimentation because of their wide applicability and the better results they give'. This is clearly one of the many problems (factory farming is another) on which the Christian's moral judgments must be informed by the most reliable evidence he can gain from the scientists and technologists.

[3] Quoted in *Crusade*, May 1973.

Bad stewardship

To conclude from this, however, that all we need to resolve the ecological crisis is better science and more efficient technology is a gross over-simplification. When the Christian looks out on the world around him, what impresses him most is not bad technology, but bad stewardship. Instead of restrained conservation of natural resources, he sees greedy squandering for short-term gain. Instead of fair distribution of food for the benefit of all mankind, he finds that one in five people in Britain suffer from obesity while thousands of Asians starve. Future generations are forgotten in the rush to live better now. Who cares whether the world's supply of fossil fuels will run out in a decade or two, provided there is enough petrol to make the motor-mower go this summer? What does deforestation in Brazil matter so long as our Sunday papers are not cut in size? Whether or not technology comes up with effective substitutes for petrol and paper, these basic human attitudes of mind will prove decisive factors in man's fight against famine and shortage.

Economic considerations underlie many ecological problems, and human greed is nowhere more obvious than in the business of maximizing profits. If there is a good market for white veal, some farmers will always be found who are prepared to deprive their calves of light and straw in order to supply the demand. Sometimes the influences are more subtle. Industrialists who are forced by law to swallow their own smoke (or to use combustible, but more expensive, packaging materials) may well find themselves priced out of competition by foreign competitors, and no nation wishes to lower its living standards by putting its businessmen at a disadvantage with others. National selfishness, therefore, can be as big an obstacle to environmental purity as personal greed. Speaking about the difficulties involved in controlling pollution of the Rhine internationally, Lord Kennet (who for two years held special governmental responsibility for the environment) commented: 'human nature and organized human cupidity are such that even so simple a thing cannot be regulated simply.'[4]

Technology can improve human living conditions, but it has no power to change human nature. When, therefore, a man like Sir Peter Medawar states bluntly at a meeting of the British Association for the Advancement of Science that 'the deterioration of the environment produced by technology is a technological problem for which technology has found, is finding and will continue to find solutions',[5] the Christian remains sceptical. Science has no answer to the moral problems of greed and selfishness.

The Christian gospel, however, does provide such an answer, because it deals with the spiritual and moral nature of man in a radical way. It is when technological expertise is wedded to the moral power-supply of the Holy Spirit that the potential for change becomes enormous.

This is not to pretend that all Christians are first-class conservationists. Most of us share to some extent in the Pharisees' fault of overlooking in ourselves the faults which we energetically condemn in others. It is one thing, for example, to deplore the fact that such a tiny proportion of the gross national product is spent on aid to developing countries, and quite another to think hard about cancelling an expensive summer holiday. Campaigning for famine relief is so much easier than eating less oneself. Anson Mount, religious editor of *Playboy* magazine, once countered a charge of sexual immorality by drawing attention to Christian over-eating. 'If I know my Christian theology,' he argued, 'gluttony is just as serious a personal sin as any of the other possible intemperate indulgences. And I see dozens of fat ladies walking down the streets with no apparent guilt on their countenances . . . I know a 300-pound archbishop! But I've never heard anybody challenge his moral integrity.'[6]

[4] Lord Kennet, *Controlling our Environment*, p. 16.
[5] Quoted in *The Times*, 4 September 1969.
[6] Quoted by F. Ridenour, *It all Depends* (G/L Publications, 1969), p. 228.

Mount was, of course, trying to squeeze out of a tight corner by changing the subject (Hugh Hefner did not build up his *Playboy* empire on glossy fold-out pictures of fat archbishops), but the criticism is a valid one. Christians cannot expect to gain a hearing on any moral issue if they are inconsistent in the way they live. Significantly, all the New Testament's teaching on stewardship is directed at believers. As well as campaigning for environmental improvements, and encouraging the government to resist the existentialist mood of living only for the present, Christian stewards will therefore make sure that their own house is in order – even if this means a cut in their standard of living, or a restriction in the size of their families.

The humanist's dilemma, as he faces a world in which man has so much power and so little control, is very well summed up in Edmund Leach's book *A Runaway World?* 'Men have become like gods,' he writes. 'Isn't it about time that we understood our divinity? Science offers us total mastery over our environment and over our destiny, yet instead of rejoicing we are deeply afraid. Why should this be?'[7]

The Christian reply is that man is afraid of his own human nature, and very rightly so. The story of the nuclear bomb shows how deeply engrained is man's instinct to abuse great power, and there are few sights more frightening than the mushroom cloud. Only as people are released by the gospel of Christ from this inner tendency to abuse and destroy will the prospect of a better environment become more than a pipe-dream. The sensitive Christian will therefore hear a clear call to communicate his faith in resolution 6 of the 1968 Lambeth Conference: 'The Conference urges all Christians, in obedience to the doctrine of creation, to take all possible action to ensure man's responsible stewardship over nature; in particular in his relationship with animals,

[7] E. Leach, *A Runaway World?* (BBC Publications, 1968), p. 1.

and with regard to the conservation of the soil, and the prevention of pollution of air, soil and ocean.'

Questions for discussion

1. How high on your scale of priorities would you place concern for the environment? How can the individual express his concern best?

2. 'When will we reach the point that hunting, the pleasure in killing animals for sport, will be regarded as a mental aberration?' Do you agree with the sentiment that underlies this question of Albert Schweitzer's?

3. Do you agree that the idea of stewardship offers a Christian solution to the problems of a misused, polluted environment? If not, what alternatives would you suggest?

For further reading

F. A. Schaeffer, *Pollution and the Death of Man* (Hodder, 1970)
J. W. Klotz, *Ecology Crisis* (Concordia, 1972)
H. Montefiore, *Can Man Survive?* (Fontana, 1970)

3 ABORTION

'How would you like to see a horse with a green tail?' asked the soldier. The 14-year-old girl, who had been walking past the Guards Barracks with a group of friends, allowed herself to be drawn inside. She was taken into a room, and there raped by several guardsmen. Later, as the result of her horrifying ordeal, she was admitted to hospital in a state of physical and emotional collapse, pregnant; and it was in this condition that an obstetrician called Aleck Bourne found her.

After a week, during which he kept the girl under close observation, Bourne came to a conclusion that was to put his whole professional career in jeopardy. On the eighth day, he operated to terminate her pregnancy. This, as he well knew, was against the law, and when two policemen arrived to seek evidence from the girl against the soldiers, he told them what he had done and sat back to await the consequences. He did not have to wait long. In due course he was formally charged with using an instrument to procure a miscarriage.

The law of the land

The trial of Aleck Bourne made legal history in Britain, mainly because of the judge's interpretation of the law in his summing up. Mr Justice Macnaughten ruled that the provision of the Infant Life Preservation Act of 1929, that 'no act shall be punishable when done in good faith with the intention of saving the life of the mother', covered therapeutic abortion. He also gave it as his opinion that 'saving the life of the mother' included the preservation of her physical and mental health. 'If the doctor is of the opinion', he directed the jury, 'that the probable consequence of the continuation of the pregnancy would indeed make the woman a physical wreck, or a mental wreck, then he operated, in that honest belief, for the purpose of preserving the life of the mother.'

It was in 1938 that Bourne was tried and acquitted, and in retrospect it seems amazing that for thirty years the legality of every therapeutic abortion conducted in British hospitals hung on the slender thread of that single legal precedent. During this time, pressure gradually mounted for further reform. The scandal of back-street abortions (estimated by some to be running at the rate of 100,000 a year) pricked the public conscience more and more sharply. In the early '60s there was a flutter of attempted legislation; and eventually, in 1967, the Liberal MP David Steel succeeded in gaining Parliament's approval for his Bill 'to amend and clarify the law relating to the termination of pregnancy by registered medical practitioners'.

The 1967 Abortion Act legalizes abortion when two doctors believe '(a) that the continuance of the pregnancy would involve risk to the life of the pregnant woman, or of injury to the physical or mental health of the pregnant woman or any existing children of her family, greater than if the pregnancy were terminated; *or* (b) that there is a substantial risk that if the child were born it would suffer from such physical or mental abnormalities as to be seriously handicapped'.

The Act also stipulates that abortions must be carried out by registered medical practitioners at hospitals or clinics approved by the Ministry of Health; and there is a conscience clause included for the benefit of those who are opposed to abortion on principle.

The heat of the battles which raged around the passage of David Steel's Bill through Parliament did not dissipate nearly so quickly as its supporters would have liked. If numbers are any indication of success, the Act has certainly succeeded in making abortions more readily available (the annual figure rose from 33,598 legal operations in 1968-9 to over 200,000 in 1973-4, but there is little evidence to show that the number of back-street terminations has dropped correspondingly. One foreseeable complication has been that many pregnant girls who would prefer an NHS termination are driven to private clinics through lack of hospital beds, and in the private sector they inevitably fall prey to abortionists who will operate only at an astronomical price. A Nurse Teacher from London reported in a Gallup Poll survey that she had known gynaecologists 'clap their pockets and wink when they speak of their "private patients" '.[1] Professor Hugh McLaren of Birmingham University concludes, sadly, that 'the Act has made prostitutes out of some doctors and lowered the ethical standards in parts of the medical profession as low as they can go'.[2]

No doubt such criticisms apply only to a tiny minority of medical men, but the pressures on obstetricians and gynaecologists are formidable and increasing. Some doctors find that if they appeal to the conscience clause in the Act they can forget about all prospects of promotion. One such applicant was advised by a selection committee to 'cut his losses and emigrate'.[3] Nursing staff find themselves in similar difficulties if they voice conscientious objections to abortion. In January 1973 a 46-year-old theatre superintendent felt obliged to leave her Liverpool hospital because, as she said, 'we were put under such pressure to assist in the operations that life became extremely unpleasant. One gynaecologist told us that if we didn't assist then we would have to look for

[1] Gallup Poll survey on the opinion of hospital nurses on the working of the Abortion Act, 1972.

[2] Sunday Telegraph article, 'Abortion: a Profitable Business'.

[3] From a letter (signed) in the British Medical Journal, October 1972.

45

another job'.[4] Eleven other nurses, the majority of the hospital's theatre nursing staff, resigned with her in protest.

Perhaps the most unpleasant feature of life under the 1967 Act has been the mushrooming of abortion referral bureaux. These middle-men, who ironically owe their success to the ethical standards of the General Medical Council which forbid doctors to advertise or to canvass for patients, exist to put pregnant girls in touch with abortion clinics. Although the Department of Health now requires licensed clinics not to accept patients from bureaux that 'advertise abroad or employ touts', it is hard to see how this kind of directive can be enforced. The inevitable result has been that abortion fees are pushed still higher, while the provisions of the Act that a woman must have carefully assessed grounds for termination are brushed aside. A *Sunday Telegraph* investigation team found that same-day abortions could be arranged for foreign girls who quite literally dropped from the skies and arrived on a bureau's doorstep with no more introduction than a taxi tout at London Airport.

The outworking of the Abortion Act has not therefore been an unqualified success story. Mainly as a result of these criticisms, and at the prompting of 256 MPs who signed a motion calling for an enquiry, the government appointed a Committee in 1971 to investigate the working of the Act, under the chairmanship of Mrs Justice Lane.[5] Although the Lane Committee's terms of reference were restricted to an examination of the way the law works (and specifically excluded any redrafting of the grounds on which abortions may be obtained), the basic ethical issues have once more been pushed to the forefront, and the opinions of all interested parties canvassed. So again the question is raised – what special contribution, if any, has the Christian to make to the contemporary abortion debate?

[4] Reported in *The Daily Mail*, 22 January 1973.
[5] The Lane Committee submitted its Report in April 1974.

Moral considerations

The answer lies along three main lines. Because (particularly for the Christian) every woman who asks for an abortion is a person in need, not a cold statistic in an annual report, the demands of *compassion* must be satisfied. Then, at a more theoretical level, important questions have to be asked about the *sanctity of human life*. Is abortion merely an extension of contraception, or does the deliberate destruction of a foetus amount to murder? Finally, conflicting views about the *quality of life* are expressed by those who take sides in the abortion debate, and these need to be identified and assessed.

1. Compassion

If Aleck Bourne had been asked in 1938 just *why* he chose to risk his career by operating on his 14-year-old patient, 'compassion' might have been his brief reply. As a qualified gynaecologist with the skill and resources to end a young girl's misery, he just could not stand by her bedside, shrug his shoulders, and say, 'I'm sorry, my dear, but the law won't allow me to help you.' Some might argue that the girl deserved to be in the predicament in which she found herself, but if Bourne's compassion had not reached beyond the demands of strict justice it would hardly have matched the compassionate love of Jesus which took him to the cross for sinners. And Christ's example provides the only firm standard by which a Christian can measure compassion. Repeatedly, the Gospel writers tell us how Jesus was 'moved with compassion' for the disabled, the bereaved, the harassed and the helpless;[6] and as Rex Gardner, a Christian gynaecologist, aptly puts it,[7] there are few people so harassed and helpless as 'the haggard, anaemic woman with two or three infants hanging whimpering on to her patched skirt long

[6] *E.g.* Mt. 9:36; 14:14; Mk. 1:41; Lk. 7:13.
[7] R. F. R. Gardner, *Abortion: The Personal Dilemma* (Paternoster, 1972), p. 165.

past bedtime', pleading for relief from her latest pregnancy. Wherever the blame lies, to take an ice-cold decision on the deeply personal problem of a distressed girl without any heart-felt expression of tenderness is a sheer impossibility for anyone fired with the compassion of Jesus.

Supporters of abortion law reform would argue that the 1967 Act, by allowing women to have their pregnancies terminated on health or social grounds, opens up new channels for compassion. In days when health is measured positively in terms of well-being rather than negatively as absence of disease, it certainly does not seem very compassionate to force a girl to bear a child which will strain her physical and mental stamina, and perhaps threaten the stability of a home in which finance, bedroom accommodation and affection are stretched to their limits. Nor does it seem enough to comfort a girl who has contracted German measles during the early stages of her pregnancy by assuring her that, in spite of her anguish at the thought of bearing an imperfect child, she is unlikely to die in childbirth and therefore does not really need an abortion.

In such circumstances it is even arguable that abortion is in the unborn child's best interests as well as its mother's. Better not to be born at all than to be born physically deformed or mentally deficient. And to be born physically and mentally whole, but unwanted and unloved, is hardly preferable. Nature, it is pointed out, already provides a natural form of miscarriage to deal with many imperfect foetuses. Is it not a right extension of this creation principle for man to use his God-given knowledge and skills to do more perfectly what nature does in a hit or miss fashion – in much the same way as a surgeon operates to deal with diseases with which the body's natural defences cannot cope?

Some would go further still, and claim that abortion is in the best interests of society too. Unlike Bible times, when every new birth represented a gain to the community, babies are now an embarrassment to an overcrowded world. In a much-publicized paper read at a Planned Parenthood

Federation Conference in 1969, Professor P. J. Huntingford drew attention to the staggering forecast that if the world's population continues to grow at its present rate there will be more people alive in 1980 than have died throughout the whole course of history before.[8] Dr John Robinson of Cambridge is quite clear what the Christian's response to the population explosion should be. Abortion must be accepted as just one of the means by which the processes of conception and birth can be controlled. 'To refuse to control or reverse them', he writes, 'is a deliberate act of freedom, carrying with it a formidable burden of responsibility.'[9]

From whatever angle the problem is approached, then, compassion dictates abortion – or so it seems. The Christian who subscribes to a liberal abortion policy is only following the example of his Lord, who showed compassion to all-comers.

But this is far too facile a solution to satisfy the Christian conscience. Compassion, like love, is a much-abused term, and the thinking Christian will want to examine all such calls to compassion very carefully indeed before he accepts them at face value. To square with biblical standards, compassion must exhibit at least three well-defined characteristics:

a. Compassion must be genuine. This sounds too obvious to mention, but Jesus devoted many of his teaching opportunities to the unscrambling of mixed motives. No doubt it seemed obvious to most people in New Testament times that all donors to charity must be motivated by a sense of compassion for the needy (why else would they give?), but Jesus was quick to draw a distinction between the ostentatious giving of those who were really only concerned to parade their own virtues, and the genuine self-sacrifice of the bereaved woman who dropped all the money she had into

[8] P. J. Huntingford, 'The Right of the Individual to Freedom of Choice and Medical Responsibility'.

[9] J. A. T. Robinson, *Christian Freedom in a Permissive Society* (SCM, 1970), p. 62.

the collection-box (Mk. 12: 42–44). It was natural to assume that anyone who said his prayers did so from a desire to worship God, but Jesus saw – and exposed – the motives of those whose real aim in praying was not to communicate with God at all, but to impress others by a show of piety.

One wonders what the X-ray moral eyesight of Jesus would make, not only of much that passes for public worship today, but of many so-called compassionate grounds advanced for aborting unwanted pregnancies. Appeals to compassion may cover some very mixed motives. A tell-tale cartoon appeared in the medical magazine *Pulse* [1] before the Abortion Bill became law, showing two doctors leaving an abortion clinic for the bank, loaded with money. As they pass a newsvendor's stand displaying a poster which reads 'Crossman worried about "on demand" abortion', one remarks to the other, 'He simply doesn't appreciate our dedicated compassion.'

Unworthy motives hide happily beneath a cloak of superficial compassion. Is the married woman who asks for abortion on family grounds really moved with compassion for her husband and her other children, or is she simply unwilling to exchange the colour TV and the planned continental holiday for a new baby? When a student's parents persuade her to seek an abortion because 'it will wreck your future otherwise', are they really acting on her behalf in love, or are they reflecting their own sense of distaste at the thought of having the respectable family image tarnished by the arrival of an illegitimate child? These are embarrassing, painful questions, but they have to be asked if genuine compassion is to be distinguished from its plausible but counterfeit counterpart.

b. Compassion must be radical. Jesus probed into the innermost recesses of man's motivation. He also went right to the heart of human problems, and he never offered an easy

[1] *Pulse*, 3 May 1969; quoted by R. F. R. Gardner, *op. cit.*, p. 130

way out of a difficulty. Perhaps his interview with the rich young ruler illustrates this best. Mark tells us that there was compassion in Jesus' eyes as he saw through this man's dilemma (Mk. 10: 21), but the solution he offered was a painfully radical one: 'Go, sell what you have, and give to the poor, and you will have treasure in heaven; and come, follow me.' When the young man's face fell, compassion did not compel Jesus to soften his demand. To have done so might have succeeded in temporarily papering over the cracks in a young man's life-style, but it would have done nothing to resolve his basic need, which was to be cut free from the materialism which held him prisoner.

With true insight into the radical nature of Christian love, Rex Gardner writes: 'To abort a pregnancy because it is extra-marital may sound compassionate, but if it does nothing about the underlying problem it has no resemblance to true compassion.'[2] Psychiatrists tell us that such appeals for abortion are usually symptomatic of deeper distress, and to meet such situations as this with promises of an easily terminated pregnancy may be no solution at all. It may be an evasion of the real problem. To remove a painful symptom is not compassionate if the disease itself is left untreated. When young girls return to gynaecological wards for their third and fourth terminations, the indications are that abortion is being used as a palliative, while the underlying moral and spiritual condition still festers below the surface.

Abortion may not be in the best long-term interests of a married woman either, even though her pregnancy causes her a great deal of distress. One nursing sister, still in her early thirties, wrote from the north of England: 'Four years ago I found I was expecting my fourth baby, with my youngest child being then fourteen months old and the eldest four years. I was very depressed and under a great strain. I even contemplated an abortion, seeing two doctors for their permission. I was told that they felt I could go through with

[2] R. F. R. Gardner, *Abortion: The Personal Dilemma*, p. 131.

it. It has been a struggle, but looking back I realize how lucky I was that these doctors took the decision and did not let me have an abortion. My little boy now aged four years is adorable. . . . '[3]

In this case at least the decision not to terminate the pregnancy, though distressing at the time, turned out to be a compassionate refusal. Among gynaecologists who testify that they have known many unwanted pregnancies, but few unwanted babies, is Aleck Bourne himself, the man who sparked off the demands for a more liberal abortion policy. In his memoirs, Bourne (who has now deserted the ranks of the Abortion Law Reform Association to become an executive committee member of the Society for the Protection of the Unborn Child) writes: 'During my long years in practice I have had many a letter of the deepest gratitude for refusing to accede to an early appeal.'[4]

Furthermore, there is increasing evidence of post-operative physical and psychological damage following abortions. Myre Sim, a consultant psychiatrist, reports that he has had to treat twenty-three patients with post-abortive mental illnesses since 1963, the majority of them after the passing of the Abortion Act, as against only three during the preceding twelve years.[5] And in a comment on a research paper by Arthur and Margaret Wynn which draws attention to the physical dangers involved in terminating pregnancies, Sir John Peel, the Queen's gynaecologist, admits: 'I have no doubt whatever that there is a percentage of serious consequences, particularly on patients who are having their first pregnancy terminated.'[6]

Christian compassion, then, does not always dictate the

[3] Gallup Poll survey, 1972.

[4] A. Bourne, *A Doctor's Creed* (Gollancz, 1963).

[5] M. Sim, *The Abortion Act: a Social Malady* (Society for the Protection of the Unborn Child, 1972).

[6] As reported in *The Daily Telegraph*, 2 March 1973. The Wynns' research was published by the Foundation for Education and Research in Child-Bearing.

line of least resistance. Because love (as the Bible defines it) means giving rather than getting, even the sacrifices involved in bringing up a deformed or defective child may bring to both mother and family positive rewards which outweigh all the disadvantages.[7] And the assumption that the handicapped enjoy life less than 'normal people' is far from being proved. To be genuine, compassion has to be radical.

c. Compassion must be all-embracing. Significantly, the only two of Jesus' parables recorded by Luke in which the word 'compassion' occurs are those of the good Samaritan and the prodigal son. In each case Jesus told the story to show how God's compassion embraces those whom others would consider 'out of bounds' as proper objects of his love. The priest's sense of compassion was apparently not touched as he hurried past the bleeding man in the gutter on the Jericho road (Lk. 10: 30 ff.), and the loyal son's sense of justice was outraged by his father's show of compassion to his worthless brother (Lk. 15: 11 ff.).

In the contemporary debate about abortion, too, there are those who tend to be ignored when compassion is being apportioned. Foremost among them is the foetus itself. It is hard to feel compassion for someone or something you have never seen. A man who takes the most stubborn stand against therapeutic abortion is likely to change his views when it is his own wife's life or health that is in danger. It is always far easier to feel compassion for someone you know than for a mere name in a case-book. Yet even names in case-books can come alive and inspire tenderness, if the cases are written up vividly enough – *far more so than the unfortunate foetus to be aborted.* The only people who actually see the foetus are the medical staff in the operating theatre, which perhaps explains why the sympathies of theatre staff are often far more with the foetus than with the patient.

The sensitivities of nurses and doctors, too, are frequently

[7] For such a positive attitude, see Dale Rogers, *Angel Unawares* (Hodder, 1953).

ignored, even though it is they who bear the main emotional trauma from repeated abortion operations. Who seriously considers the obstetrician as a candidate for compassion? Rex Gardner describes the surgeon's feelings as he begins an operation to terminate a pregnancy, in words that compel our attention: 'It is a lonely operation. Although dilatation of the cervix, the neck of the womb, is an operation he performs many times a week, on this occasion it will be different. He takes that first dilator and is tinglingly aware that he is about to seal the fate of a foetus, that he is about to alter history. In other operations the cervix will dilate up readily, but in this operation it will fight, grip the end of the dilator and force it back into his hand. And then at last he will win, and as he does so he will wonder who has lost.'[8] Terminating a *late* pregnancy can be an even more terrifying experience. A staff nurse from Scotland tells how 'a termination was carried out in a hospital where I worked. The baby was alive – it was not discovered until the baby cried in the boiler-room where it had been taken to be burned. I consider this murder. This made up my mind for all time that abortion on demand is an evil thing.'[9]

Words like these arouse our sympathies for the three gynaecological ward sisters who gave up their jobs in one teaching hospital because they felt they could no longer face the constant pressures (two of them subsequently had to seek psychiatric help).[1] They help us to understand the 'traumatic emotional effect' felt by a Senior Consultant at St Mary Abbots Hospital, Kensington, in carrying out abortions. 'To perform abortions', he told a national newspaper reporter, 'one has to be tough. It is difficult to kid yourself that you are not taking a life when you are throwing little arms, ribs and legs into a bucket.'

It is a fundamental principle of Christian ethics that people should always be treated as ends, never as means

[8] R. F. R. Gardner, *Abortion: The Personal Dilemma*, p. 14.
[9] Gallup Poll survey, 1972.
[1] Evidence submitted by a Matron to the Gallup Poll survey.

54

only. If the possibility of brutalizing the hangman is an important consideration for the Christian in making up his mind about the rights and wrongs of capital punishment, his compassionate concern in cases of abortion must extend to the doctor and the nurse as well as to everyone else involved. Compassion which is not *all-embracing* is not genuinely Christian.

2. Sanctity of life

It is, of course, a matter of dispute whether or not such compassion should rightly extend to the foetus as a human being, at all, and the teaching of Scripture on the sanctity of human life is highly relevant here.

This is a principle which underlies the biblical doctrines of creation and redemption. The cross is the measure of every man's worth in God's sight. No-one can be disposable, because the Good Shepherd who laid down his life for the sheep is also the Good Shepherd who leaves the ninety-nine in order to seek and find the lost individual (Jn. 10: 11; Lk. 15: 4 ff.). And this theme, which finds such an important place in the teaching of the New Testament, is echoed in the early chapters of Genesis. All human life is precious, because every human being bears God's image (which is why euthanasia is different from having an animal put to sleep at the vet's). 'Whoever sheds the blood of man,' God warned Noah, 'by man shall his blood be shed; for God made man in his own image' (Gn. 9: 6).

The full implication of that verse from Genesis should not escape us. Judicial shedding of blood does not infringe the principle of the sanctity of human life, according to the Old Testament; capital punishment is seen not as an infringement of life's sanctity but as a defence of it, and it is in this context that the sixth commandment of the Decalogue ('Thou shalt not kill') should be read. But what the Bible does condemn is the *unjust* taking of life, the killing of the innocent.

55

On this principle, it is very difficult to see how abortion can ever be justified. The foetus has done nothing to deserve death. Its only 'crime' is that it exists as the unwanted result of its parents' irresponsibility, and that is not sufficient reason to deprive it of its right to live.

This, however, begs the main question at issue. Is the foetus, or is it not, a human being with the same rights as its mother? If the answer is in the affirmative, abortion must be bracketed with infanticide, and highly emotive language like that used by a Lancashire lawyer in a pamphlet published shortly before the passing of the Abortion Act becomes appropriate. 'Are we still determined to uphold the sanctity of human life?' he asked. 'If the Abortion Bill goes through, Herod will laugh in Hell. There will be perpetrated in our name a Massacre of the Innocents more dreadful in its scope than any Herod could have imagined.'[2] That, of course, reflects the view of many prominent theologians (Bonhoeffer was one who regarded abortion as 'nothing but murder'[3]), and it represents the official Roman Catholic attitude towards induced abortion. In October 1970 the Pope was reported in *The Times* as saying: 'Abortion has been considered homicide since the first centuries of the Church and nothing permits it to be considered otherwise today.'

There are others, however, who look upon the status of the foetus very differently. Professor Glanville Williams of Cambridge, for example, denies that the foetus has any independent human rights at all, until it is capable of separate existence. He points out that a natural miscarriage is not regarded by anyone as the death of a human being. 'A foetus that is spontaneously aborted before the end of the seventh month can be burned in the back garden or put into a hospital incinerator . . . Even the Catholics who now generally maintain that this foetus has a soul, do not perform a funeral service . . . By what freak of logic, then, can we assert that if

[2] E. Ainsworth, *To Be or Not to Be* (privately published, 1967).
[3] D. Bonhoeffer, *Ethics* (Fontana, 1964), p. 176.

56

the abortion is deliberately induced the foetus becomes a person?"[4] On this view, disposing of a foetus becomes no more or less immoral than getting rid of a nagging appendix, and abortion is bracketed with contraception, not infanticide. 'The question', writes John Robinson, 'revolves around the prevention or suspension of pregnancy. And the first thing to recognize is that the line between the two is arbitrary . . . Conception is being seen to be such a continuous process that at what stage one intercepts it is . . . a matter of relative indifference.'[5]

For centuries, Christian and secular opinion has see-sawed between these two extreme positions. Augustine tried to pinpoint the time of the foetus's 'animation' (after which it had full human rights) as between thirty and forty days after conception for a male, and between the sixtieth and eightieth day for a female. In British law this became identified with the mother's experience of 'quickening', so that before 1837 a pregnant woman could be hanged if her foetus was 'inanimate', but not if it had become 'animate'.

With advances in embryology, and the discovery that quickening does not correspond with any particular point in the development of the foetus, the test of viability has been substituted for animation. But even this does not provide us with foolproof solutions, because the increased sophistication of life-support systems enables foetuses to survive outside the womb at earlier and earlier stages of pregnancy. In America, a baby of twenty-three weeks' gestation has been kept alive. Under British law, at present, abortions may be carried out until the twenty-eighth week (between April 1968 and May 1971, 3,611 pregnancies were terminated after the twentieth week in England and Wales), which means that if a woman is genuinely ill and delivery is induced before the twenty-eighth week, everything possible may be done to save her baby; but if the child is unwanted, it can be dumped in a

---

[4] Glanville Williams, Introduction to A. Jenkins, *Law for the Rich* (Riband Books, 1964), pp. 16f.

[5] J. A. T. Robinson, *Christian Freedom in a Permissive Society*, pp. 53, 61.

plastic bag destined for the incinerator. Such a situation is not only anomalous; it lays an impossible burden on the medical staff involved.

The Bible is silent about the rights and wrongs of abortion as such, but it does provide valuable guide-lines to help Christians arrive at a right attitude towards the unborn child. For one thing, it is clear from Scripture that human personality is ante-natal. 'Before I formed you in the womb', God assured Jeremiah, 'I knew you' (Je. 1: 5). Clearly Jeremiah's mother would have lost more than an insignificant blob of foetal jelly if her pregnancy had been terminated. Ecclesiastes 11: 5 preserves another interesting comment on the beginning of life: 'As you do not know how the spirit comes to the bones in the womb of a woman with child, so you do not know the work of God who makes everything.' The same theme shines through the poetic language of Psalm 139: 'Thou didst form my inward parts, thou didst knit me together in my mother's womb . . . My frame was not hidden from thee, when I was being made in secret . . Thy eyes beheld my unformed substance; in thy book were written, every one of them, the days that were formed for me, when as yet there was none of them' (Ps. 139: 13–16; cf. Jb. 10:8 ff.).

This kind of language is a far cry from the rather cynical view of those who attribute the beginning of any new life to a one-in-a-million chance meeting of sperm and egg. However we weight these verses, God clearly plans pregnancies (cf. Ru. 4: 13; 1 Sa. 1: 19; Lk. 1: 13, 31). He must also foresee miscarriages.

If we piece this biblical teaching together, it is clear that the protection which the sanctity of life principle gives to every living human being must extend to the life of the foetus too. Nothing less will do justice to God's concern and purpose for the unborn child. So we cannot agree either with the Abortion Law Reform Association that the foetus is just part of the mother's body (and therefore within her rights to nurture or destroy, just as she likes), nor with Dr

58

Robinson when he claims that abortion is nothing more than a birth control device.

This is not to say that the bringing up of an unwanted baby should be laid on the parents as some kind of punishment (that would be a hideous fate for the child as well as for the adults), but with so many childless couples queueing to adopt, it does mean that a pregnant girl should be encouraged to go to full term, whether she wants to or not, out of sheer respect for the foetal life she bears. A foetus is too precious to be discarded simply because it is inconvenient. The Christian attitude to the unborn child, therefore, must be to defend its right to live and develop, and to lay the burden of proof to the contrary squarely on the shoulders of those who would wish to set that right aside.

3. Quality of life

There is one Old Testament passage which appears to teach a difference in value between the life of a woman and that of her unborn child. Exodus 21: 22f. lays down that if a pregnant woman becomes involved in a fight between men, with the result that she loses her baby but is otherwise unharmed, those responsible should pay an appropriate fine. If, however, the woman dies, then the punishment must be 'life for life'. In other words, the price of a foetus can be calculated in cash, but the value of a woman can only be measured in terms of life. So there does seem to be a difference in value, in the eyes of God's law, between a mother-to-be and her unborn child.

We must be cautious in applying the details of Old Testament legislation to modern life-situations, but the principle underlying this law encourages us to conclude that when there is a clash of life-interest between mother-to-be and unborn child, saving the life of the woman must take priority. As a mature person, her right to life must be put before the survival of her foetus, especially if she has wider responsibilities as a wife and mother of other children.

Many Christians would go a step further and say (with

the judge in the Bourne case) that the protection of a girl's life involves preserving her mental and physical health, as well as saving her from death. The Bible certainly sees life qualitatively as well as quantitatively, which lends some support to this view. Nevertheless, at this point the Christian wants to move more cautiously than some. In 1969–70, 93 per cent of all registered abortions were carried out on health grounds, which itself suggests that this section of the Act has been interpreted far too loosely; and that is a suspicion backed up by those with experience in gynaecological units. A Working Party of the Royal College of Obstetricians and Gynaecologists noted that in the majority of cases where abortion was recommended on grounds of health risk, the indications were purely social, with no real danger of mental or physical injury to the woman at all. One student at a Teaching Hospital commented bluntly: ' "Psychological grounds" seems to cover almost everything.'[6]

If the Christian is disturbed (as he should be) by the very low value this definition of sickness places on the lives of unborn children, he is equally appalled by the assumption of the pro-abortion lobby that they can decide whether another person's life is worth living or not. 'Miss X caught German measles early in her pregnancy; the baby may be born blind or deaf; far better, surely, to finish it off now than let it enter life under those physical disadvantages – plus the social stigma of illegitimacy?' 'Mrs Y's family resources are stretched to breaking-point already, and now she is pregnant again; she'd be well advised to have an abortion – after all, she'll never be able to make the poor little thing's life worth living!'

These, and others like them, are blatant value-judgments. They are typified by the dedication on the fly-leaf of Madeleine Simms and Keith Hindell's book *Abortion Law Reformed*,[7] which reads 'To the thalidomide mothers for whom reform came too late'.

[6] Gallup Poll survey, 1972.
[7] M. Simms and K. Hindell, *Abortion Law Reformed* (Peter Owen, 1971).

The really terrifying thing about making any judgment on the value of somebody else's life is that logically there is no end to the evaluating process. The implication is that the deaf, the blind, the lame and the socially superfluous are disposable; and it is only a short step from disposable foetuses to disposable people. If life is without value for a foetus which may be born deformed or deficient, why not end the miserable existence of those who *become* deformed or deficient in later life? Judged by eugenic standards, most of us are imperfect specimens anyway.

The assumption that the quality of life enjoyed by a deformed or socially deprived child is valueless, is something the Christian has to challenge. Who is to say that the life of a thalidomide victim is not worth living, either from his own point of view, his family's, or the community's? The Bible has a great deal to say about the severely handicapped – including the blind, the deaf, the dumb and the mutilated. It even speaks of the morally sick (a dimension often missing from modern debates about abortion). But the attitude Scripture encourages the healthy and whole to adopt towards the lame ducks of this life is not to put them 'compassionately' out of their misery, but to treat them with all the more respect and extra care as valued members of the community, strengthened by the assurance that the rest of the family and community will themselves benefit from the opportunities thus gained to serve others in practical love.

The Bible has the highest view of physical well-being and material goods as precious gifts from God to man, but it never suggests that the value of life automatically drops with the coming of material hardship or social deprivation. 'I have learned, in whatever state I am, to be content,' writes Paul. 'I know how to be abased, and I know how to abound; in any and all circumstances I have learned the secret of facing plenty and hunger, abundance and want' (Phil. 4: 11, 12). The key to human happiness and a valuable life does not lie in health and wealth, according to the Bible, but in a close relationship with God (Ps. 16: 11).

61

There is no convenient set of proof-texts the Christian can trot out to resolve every abortion problem. Sometimes he will be as torn and puzzled as anyone else, when asked to advise or decide on a particular case. But in all cases he will try to uphold these three main-line biblical principles. *The sanctity of human life* must be safeguarded against those who would cheapen it. *Quality of life* must never be measured in a way that labels the deficient and deprived as disposable. And *compassion* must be Christ-like – genuine, radical and all-embracing.

Questions for discussion

1. Do some social pressures (*e.g.* family problems) justify abortion?

2. In cases where a baby is likely to be born physically deformed or mentally defective, would you advise the mother-to-be to press for an abortion?

3. If abortion is to be ruled out as an acceptable method of birth control, should contraceptives be made more readily available to the general public to curb the number of unwanted babies in the world?

For further reading

O. O'Donovan, *The Christian and the Unborn Child* (Grove Press, 1973)

R. F. R. Gardner, *Abortion* (Paternoster, 1972)

W. O. Spitzer and C. L. Saylor (eds.), *Birth Control and the Christian* (Coverdale, 1969)

4 DIVORCE

'Marriage', said the humorist, 'is like a besieged city. All those outside want to get in – and all those inside want to get out.'

Cynical though this view may sound, the statistics support it. Marriage as an institution has never been more popular. From the latest official figures it seems that only five out of every hundred girls can now expect to be unmarried by the time they are forty-five, and one sociologist writing in *New Society* has gone so far as to describe the growing popularity of marriage among young people as 'one of the most significant social features of modern Britain'. In some American universities one-third of the students on the campus are married, and student marriage is a phenomenon British educationalists, too, are having to take seriously in their planning. One recent survey showed that more than 40 per cent of the British students interviewed thought it was 'a good idea' to get married while still at college. With the trend to marry younger, and with the rejection of the old-fashioned idea that every young man should be in a position to support his bride financially before popping the question (a shift of opinion that would have shocked grandfather – and one or two fathers too, if the truth be known), the pressures on student married accommodation are bound to increase even more in the very near future.

Perhaps, though, the greatest tribute of all to the institution of marriage comes from the divorcees, three-quarters of whom choose to get married again after the failure of their first attempt. The principle of 'once bitten, twice shy' obviously does not apply in this sector of life.

Nevertheless, although marriage is booming, the divorce rate is climbing even more steeply. While registrars were coping with 58,000 more marriages in 1971 than they were a decade earlier, solicitors were experiencing a similar increase in divorce petitions over a period of just three years (110,895 in 1971 as against 55,057 in 1968). So the statistics show that at a time when more and more people want to marry, fewer and fewer couples are managing to stay married successfully.

There are many factors which help to account for this apparently curious situation. Prominent among modern pressures on the permanence of marriage, the sociologists tell us, is the increasing independence of women. In Bible times a divorced woman normally had to remarry for sheer economic survival (which is why we do not find the modern distinction between divorce and legal separation in the Bible), but today education and job opportunities are such that no woman who chooses to leave her husband need fear starvation. And the emancipation of the wife has its side-effects too. Along with the increasing number of working wives, aids to housekeeping have multiplied. An Eskimo husband may still miss his wife if she is not at home in the evening to chew his boots, but a British male can get along fairly happily without a home-maker to help him. With the launderette round the corner and precooked food in the supermarket, he may miss a wife's companionship, but he will not lack very much in the way of material comforts she might provide. And when we add to this the fact that married life is no longer seen as the only acceptable setting for sexual intimacy (or for childbearing, for that matter), the task of *staying* married begins to look more and more formidable.

The law of the land

Changes in the law have also made divorce decrees easier to obtain. Before the middle of the nineteenth century the only concession the man-in-the-street could hope to gain, if he wanted to end his marriage, was a legal separation. Even at this time it was technically possible for an individual to get a divorce by having a special Act of Parliament passed in his favour (317 people managed to do this in the course of two centuries), but it was not until 1857 that the Matrimonial Causes Act allowed full divorce in cases of adultery. Since then, following the trend in public opinion, there has been a gradual relaxing of controls. The Herbert Act extended the grounds of divorce in 1937 to include desertion, cruelty and incurable insanity; and William Wilson's Divorce Reform Bill of 1969 proposed even more sweeping changes. This Bill became the law of the land effectively at the beginning of 1971, and its provisions are worth looking at in a little more detail.

The new Act *alters the grounds on which divorce may be granted.* This is a radical change. Since 1971, a petitioner does not have to prove that his or her partner has committed a matrimonial offence (adultery, cruelty or desertion). All he has to do is to show, to the court's satisfaction, that the marriage has broken down irretrievably. The terms 'guilty partner' and 'innocent partner', therefore, drop out of divorce law terminology altogether. A divorce decree now sets out to do nothing more than state a fact – that the marriage relationship is dead. It is no longer part of the court's task to apportion blame. And, as evidence of irretrievable breakdown, the court may accept, in addition to proven adultery, cruelty or desertion, a period of separation which must be at least two years if both parties agree that the marriage should be ended, or at least five if one of them dissents.

Although this last provision of the Act has been dubbed a 'Casanova's Charter', there is much here that should meet

5

with Christian approval. At least theoretically, the new law makes divorce harder by substituting 'irretrievable break-down' for the matrimonial offence. A single act of adultery, for example, which would automatically have resulted in the granting of a decree under the old legislation, may now do so no longer if the court decides that it has not broken the marriage bond irretrievably. The Christian also has some sympathy with the move to cut out all reference to guilty and innocent partners. No-one can regret the departure of the contrived matrimonial offence, with the private investi-gator lurking ostentatiously behind the curtain, complete with his little camera to provide the court with the necessary evidence. It must be counted to the new Act's credit that it has made this particularly sordid route to divorce a thing of the past. Many so-called 'innocent' husbands and wives were in fact as morally blameworthy as their partners whom the law labelled as 'guilty'.

The other section of the Act which is of particular interest is *its provision to encourage reconciliation.* Under the old law, once a couple had decided to get a divorce, it was senseless of them to try to make things up. If they did make a further attempt to live together (and it failed to work out), their action was held to condone the matrimonial offence and their case was prejudiced. So the old law tended to dis-courage reconciliation. Under the new Act, on the other hand, an estranged husband and wife whose case is before the court can live together for as long as six months, without incurring any legal disqualification if, after that time, one or other of them decides to resume divorce proceedings. In addition, the law now requires every petitioner's solicitor to discuss with him (or her) the possibilities of a reconcili-ation, and to provide a list of names and addresses of local reconciling agencies.

There are, therefore, positive attractions in the new Divorce Act for those who are concerned to preserve the stability of marriage. If nothing else, the provisions for reconciliation should stimulate Christians to involve them-

66

selves in local marriage guidance councils, and encourage local solicitors to interpret this section of the Act with insight and enthusiasm. One wonders, for example, how many names of church ministers appear on these solicitors' lists. The minister who prepared a couple for their wedding day might well be the very best 'reconciling agency' to help resolve their differences – if only they could be encouraged to see him again.

At the same time, it would be foolish to pretend that the effect of the law has been other than to make divorce easier. The offer of an end to married life after only two years is a big temptation to those who are more prone to take the easy way out than to redouble their efforts to make a difficult marriage work. Even the provisions for reconciliation, important as they are, really come too late. By the time a couple get to a solicitor's office, attitudes have hardened. Things have been done, and words said, which make reconciliation as hard as squeezing toothpaste back into the tube. And the statistics support this rather gloomy view of the new law's effect upon marriage. The number of those wanting to dissolve or annul their marriages shot up from 71,661 in 1970 to 110,895 in 1971, the first full year in which the act was operative.[1]

Divorce in the churches

1. The traditional view
A great deal of traditional Christian opinion takes a very firm line against divorce. The church may have been right, it is admitted, to encourage the state to adopt 'irretrievable breakdown' as the best basis for a fair divorce law in a secular society, but when the institution of marriage is

[1] The 1971 figures included, of course, many petitioners who had been separated for years without hope of divorce before the new Act was passed. The exact extent of the upward trend will not become clear for some time yet.

under such heavy fire, and all the trend-setting media present divorce as nothing more than a casual incident ruffling the smoothness of life's surface, Christians must do everything in their power to make divorce harder, not easier. Surely nothing less can do justice to the teaching of Jesus, who himself branded remarriage after divorce as adultery (Mk. 10: 11). As Helen Oppenheimer comments, the church 'can hardly give its formal blessing to people when they are actually doing what Christ particularly wished them not to do'.[2] In the face of Jesus' clear condemnations, the very thought of Christians advocating divorce and remarriage must smack of hypocritical double-think to an unbiased observer.

Some would go even further and argue that divorce is not only wrong on Christian grounds, but impossible. When Jesus interpreted the words of Genesis to mean that a married couple 'are no longer two but one', and followed this up by warning his disciples, 'What therefore God has joined together, let not man put asunder' (Mt. 19: 6), he was simply stating a fact of life in the plainest words he could find. No human divorce court can undo a marriage bond that has been tied by God. A divorce nisi is therefore as ineffectual as a solemn declaration by the Prime Minister that the moon is made of green cheese, and those who rely upon it are simply acting out a fiction. They can never 'remarry' in God's eyes (until death intervenes), because their marriage bond is indissoluble.

It is usually assumed that Roman Catholics bear the most vigorous witness to the doctrine of the indissolubility of marriage, but this can be a misleading impression. Certainly (despite liberal rumblings at the last Vatican Council) no Roman Catholic can ever hope to gain his church's blessing on divorce, but not *all* marriages are *true* marriages in the eyes of the Vatican. If the original wedding ceremony was not conducted by a priest, for example, the marriage is not 'sacramental' and may therefore be declared invalid by the

[2] H. Oppenheimer, *Law and Love* (Faith Press, 1962), p. 78.

church authorities if one of the partners is a Roman Catholic. Another possible ground for nullity arises if both partners are determined never to have intercourse without contraceptives. In a booklet on *Matrimony and Nullity* published by the Catholic Truth Society, Dom Peter Flood writes: 'If two parties entered into marriage with the definite condition that they would never have normal intercourse but would always practise contraceptive intercourse, such a condition might completely invalidate the contract.'[3]

It sometimes happens, then, that a marriage which has been terminated to the civil law's satisfaction in the divorce court may be declared null by Roman Catholic ecclesiastical authority – leaving each partner free to remarry with the blessing of both church and state. 'In some circumstances', admits Peter Flood, 'as where a marriage is evidently invalid in the sight of God, the Church may advise the parties to free themselves from the disabilities that they have incurred in civil law by the original contract, and therefore will permit them to proceed to a civil divorce for that purpose.'[4] So a Roman Catholic divorcee who seeks remarriage will find the church door securely locked and bolted against him; but on it, if he looks carefully, he may see a small notice which says 'Please come round the back'.

Without doubt, the chief bastion against divorce and remarriage in contemporary society is the official stand taken by the Church of England. Anglican clergy in Britain, although they may lawfully marry divorcees in church, are strongly persuaded by their bishops not to do so. The words of a special Commission which reported to Convocation in 1932 still express the official Anglican position; marriage, says the report, 'not only *ought not* to be dissolved, but also involves a moral and spiritual bond which *cannot* be finally terminated save by death'.[5] As recently as 1971, Chancellor

[3] Dom P. Flood, *Matrimony and Nullity* (Catholic Truth Society, 1968), p. 12.
[4] *Ibid.*, p. 18.
[5] Convocation Report, *The Church and Marriage*, p. 18 (italics mine).

Garth Moore could state bluntly that the doctrine of the Church of England rules out remarriage after divorce altogether. 'Though a marriage is made by the mutual act of the parties,' he wrote in a Lambeth Tract, 'upon its creation a relationship is created by God which is as indissoluble as the relationship between parent and child or brother and sister. A child may be separated from the parent; but the relationship still exists. A husband may be separated from his wife; but only death can dissolve the relationship.'[6]

This Anglican statement, however, is by no means typical of all Protestant attitudes towards divorce and remarriage. The early Reformers were willing to permit divorce on grounds of adultery, desertion and cruelty; and the Free Churches have always allowed their ministers discretion to remarry divorcees in church. Even the Church of England does not present a uniform doctrinal front. Before the Matrimonial Causes Act was passed in 1857, those who had been divorced by special Act of Parliament could be remarried according to the usual Prayer Book rite (apparently without any doctrinal scruples), and the same permission was extended after 1857 to those whom the courts exonerated as 'innocent parties'. It was not until the early twentieth century that a series of stern Lambeth Conference pronouncements set the pattern for a hardening of Anglican attitudes, and even since then, advocates of a more liberal divorce policy have not been lacking within the Church of England, as well as outside it.

2. A radical approach

The main theological argument used by those who believe divorce can sometimes be right is that *marriage is essentially a relationship*. A God-joined union is not brought about automatically, it is argued, when a clergyman or a registrar pronounces a couple man and wife on their wedding day. No

[6] G. Moore, *The Church and Marriage*, Lambeth Tract No. 2 (published by LAL, Cumberland Mansions, London).

genuine relationship can ever be imposed so superficially. Marriage is not an immediate 'being one' at all, but a gradual process of 'becoming one', as the wedding ceremony and physical intercourse are followed by a uniting of personalities. And like any relationship, a marriage may either flourish or die. As the Report of the Archbishops' Commission on *Marriage, Divorce and the Church* put it in 1971, 'Marriages vary between the heights and the depths. . . . ' They 'can be a foretaste of heaven, or an anticipation of hell'.[7] If two married people grow apart through a long period of cold indifference to such an extent that they are virtually unable to communicate with one another at any level at all, it is foolish to pretend that they are still 'one flesh', merely because a marriage certificate is tucked away in somebody's filing cabinet. Their marriage is as dead as their relationship, and the only decent thing to do with a corpse is to bury it so a new start can be made. It is a hideous charade, as well as a waste of time, to pretend that something dead is really alive.

The teaching of the Bible, it is said, supports this view of marriage as a relationship. God instituted marriage for man's good, so the lonely Adam could find help and happiness in partnership (Gn. 2: 18). To claim, therefore, as John Murray does, that even legal separation is a 'despicable expedient' for those who are called to 'discharge their marital vows and marital duties',[8] is to misunderstand God's plan for the marriage relationship entirely. A marriage which has become an intolerable burden frustrates God's purpose. It was never part of his intention that two people should have to endure grimly something which he had instituted for their happiness. Paul seems to be echoing the same theme when he reminds the Christians at Corinth that God's purpose for marriage is 'a call to live in peace'. If, in a spiritually mixed marriage, the non-Christian partner wishes to separate and finish it all, he writes, the Christian husband or

[7] *Marriage, Divorce and the Church* (SPCK, 1971), p. 26.
[8] J. Murray, *Divorce* (Presbyterian and Reformed, 1961), p. 106.

71

wife is under no compulsion to maintain the fiction of a dead relationship (1 Cor. 7: 15). It is interesting that in this context Paul calls the separated wife 'single' (verse 11) – a broad hint, perhaps, that the bond of marriage may be completely fractured by a broken relationship? Even Jesus' stern denunciations of divorce and remarriage are understandable (it is suggested), once we recognize that his aim was not to legislate for all situations, but only to expose the iniquities of those who were using the divorce law as a respectable cover in order to get rid of their unwanted partners in a cruel, high-handed way. It was these one-sided dismissals and remarriages – and only these – that Jesus condemned as adulterous.

As an exegesis of Scripture, these arguments must be taken seriously – far more so than other considerations which are sometimes brought in to give the case a boost. The Anglican Report *Putting Asunder*,[9] for example, came dangerously close to arguing that Christians should mould their thinking to modern attitudes. Its publication prompted some observers to conclude that the church, having gauged the climate of contemporary opinion, should 'examine its own practice, and even its own doctrine, accordingly'.[1] Five years later, the Commission responsible for producing *Marriage, Divorce and the Church* trod the same path of theology-by-consent, claiming that if a consensus of opinion favouring remarriage should be found in the church, it must be respected because 'at times the Church may have *moral* insight prior to and at least as fundamental as the *theological* insight necessary to explain it'.[2]

This is a dangerously misleading approach to doctrinal authority (though in other respects both Reports make valuable contributions). The Christian is called to measure contemporary opinion by biblical doctrine, not vice versa, and the teaching of the New Testament provides some very

[9] *Putting Asunder* (SPCK, 1966).
[1] *Marriage, Divorce and the Church*, p. 3.
[2] *Marriage, Divorce and the Church*, p.72 (italics mine).

72

positive guide-lines for those who are concerned to find the mind of Scripture on divorce and remarriage.

Jesus said . . .

The incident Matthew records in chapter 19 of his Gospel provides us with one penetrating insight into Jesus' attitude towards divorce. The situation was not a promising one. A group of Pharisees, intent on confounding him in debate, asked Jesus a question with a sting in its tail: 'Is it lawful to divorce one's wife *for any cause?*'

The possibility of ruling out divorce under all circumstances was not in these questioners' minds. They would assume that Jesus was not against the dissolution of marriage as such, because provisions for divorce were written right into the heart of the Old Testament law. But the *grounds* on which a divorce could be granted were a matter of conflict between rival rabbinic schools, and on this point of interpretation they hoped to lure him into a dangerous indiscretion.

The controversy centred on the wording of Deuteronomy 24: 1, a verse which laid down the proper procedure for divorce between husband and wife when 'she finds no favour in his eyes because he has found some indecency in her'. What did the law mean by 'some indecency'? Those who followed Rabbi Shammai interpreted the phrase very strictly, allowing divorce only for sexual unchastity of an extremely grave kind. 'Let a wife be as mischievous as the wife of Ahab,' said Shammai, 'she cannot be divorced except for adultery.' This, however, was far too narrow an interpretation for the disciples of Rabbi Hillel, the contemporary champions of permissiveness. They took 'some indecency' as an umbrella term to cover any and every threat to a marriage relationship. A wife who spoiled her husband's dinner (or spoke disrespectfully of her in-laws in his presence, or quarrelled so loudly that her voice could be heard next door) had given him more than adequate grounds to divorce her for 'indecency', according to Hillel.[3]

Quite deliberately, then, the Pharisees lured Jesus into a dialectical trap. Would he side with Shammai or with Hillel? Was he a conservative or a liberal? Whichever way he replied, he was bound to put himself out of favour with one influential sector of public opinion. And that was enough for the Pharisees.

Instead of answering them directly, Jesus probed behind their question. Before discussing divorce, he insisted on turning their attention to God's creation pattern for marriage. In God's ideal plan, he pointed out, there was no room for divorce at all (Mt. 19: 5, 6). 'What therefore God has joined together, let not man put asunder.'

If the Pharisees were surprised at this reply, they were quick to notice that Jesus had put his head into a convenient noose. The law of Moses clearly permitted divorce, however much dispute there might be about the grounds on which it could be granted. Was Jesus, then, denying the authority of God's revealed word (verse 7)?

After quietly pointing out that they had overstated their case (Moses *allowed* divorce; he did not command it), Jesus went on to explain the distinction he was trying to draw. He was not saying that Genesis was right and Deuteronomy wrong. The apparent conflict between these two pieces of biblical teaching arose because they were directed to very different situations. Genesis set out God's ideal plan for marriage before sin intervened to spoil all human relationships; the law of Deuteronomy, on the other hand, represented God's gracious provision for heart-hardened, sinful mankind – even though 'from the beginning it was not so' (verse 8).

Having made his explanation, Jesus went on to draw his conclusion. First, he reiterated God's creation principle:

[3] *Cf. The Babylonian Talmud in Selection* (New York, 1944), p. 178. It should be added that the administration of the divorce law was not nearly so lax as some rabbinic theory.

'whoever divorces his wife . . . and marries another, commits adultery'. Then he added his own adaptation: 'except for unchastity' (a word embracing sexual unchastity of every kind). No other Gospel writer includes this exceptive clause, and it has been variously explained away as a falsification of Jesus' teaching by those who found it too hard, or as Matthew's private addition to his source material (which comes to much the same thing), but textual evidence from the manuscripts is overwhelmingly in favour of retaining it as a genuine part of Jesus' teaching.

Three important principles emerge from this passage, all of them highly relevant to the modern divorce debate.

1. God's marriage-standards are for all men

Jesus did not draw on the creation teaching of Genesis simply to score a neat debating-point. The Pharisees had asked a question which covered the whole divorce scene (not just the more notorious cases of abuse; the word for 'divorce' is the same as that used in Mt. 1: 19 to describe Joseph's intention to 'put away' Mary when her pregnancy was discovered). Jesus responded by going back to God's creation plan for all mankind, to show that his teaching was intended to apply not just to Jewish marriage (or to Christian marriage), but to human marriage in its totality.

The implication is that God does not have different marriage standards for Christians and for non-Christians. Marriage is one of his gifts to all men, not just a private arrangement for the benefit of the Christian community. So all attempts to drive a wedge between civil marriage (which might be dissolved by divorce) and church marriage (which must be indissoluble) are unhelpful and misleading. On the practical level, such a 'solution' would no doubt put unfortunate pressures on engaged couples either to have a church wedding solely as a safeguard against desertion, or to go to a registry office so as to leave a loophole for divorce. At a theological level, this dichotomy is clearly a false one. God is not absent from a registry office wedding, even if he is not specifically invited. His extremely high marriage standards, including faithfulness and permanence, are for all men, not just for Christians.

2. *Divorce is always bad*

Similarly, it just does not square with Jesus' teaching to suggest that some divorces may be good, and others bad, according to the circumstances. If God's creation ideal leaves no room for the dissolution of marriage at all, any divorce must be bad, even though it may sometimes be justified as the least evil of all the possible courses of action a particular situation offers.

One unfortunate result of substituting the idea of irretrievable breakdown for that of the matrimonial offence is that it appears to transfer the blame for any breakdown from the couple concerned to their marriage, as though the institution of marriage can be made into some kind of third-party scapegoat on which all guilt can be laid. If the marriage itself is to blame, why should the partners feel in any way guilty as individuals? When the courts refuse to distinguish between guilt and innocence, who else can presume to point the finger of accusation at husband or wife? In so far as they are involved at all, the couple are cast as the helpless victims of circumstances; psychologically accident-prone, perhaps, in the difficult business of making relationships, but no more to blame than anyone who labours under a handicap.

The Christian has no wish to ignore psychological insights, but he is always suspicious of attempts to whitewash sin. Jesus traced the need for divorce to hardness of heart, not incapacity to relate. He labelled extra-marital sex as adultery, not as a symptom of incompatibility. The tendency to paper over the cracks of selfishness, unfaithfulness and cruelty by calling them something more polite may appeal to a modern society seeking to justify itself, but the Christian realist will not be deceived so easily. All divorce contravenes God's ideal pattern for marriage, and to pretend that the parties to it can be exonerated from all blame is little more than a deceptive bromide.

3. Marriage is not indissoluble

From the above it might seem that divorce can never be justified on Christian grounds at all. If it is always bad, how can it ever be right? That, however, was not the conclusion Jesus drew. He contrasted the Old Testament divorce law with the ideal state of affairs that existed before man's fall into sin, but he did not condemn it for that reason. And he went on to make one exception himself (but only one) to the general rule that marriage is for life.

Both the phrasing of the exceptive clause 'for unchastity' (Mt. 5: 32; 19: 9) and the social pattern of life in New Testament times show that it was full divorce Jesus had in mind here (opening up the possibility of remarriage), so it seems impossible to reconcile his words with the traditional claim that marriage is indissoluble. If 'becoming one flesh' involves a God-made union which cannot be broken under any circumstance, then Moses was mistaken in framing the divorce legislation of Deuteronomy, and Jesus was wrong to allow divorce for sexual unfaithfulness. It is interesting that Jesus took the words 'one flesh' from an Old Testament verse which embodies the biblical doctrine of marriage (Gn. 2: 24). In their Genesis context, the primary reference of these words is to sexual intercourse, which is there presented as just one of the three legs on which marriage stands (along with the social change of leaving father and mother, and 'being joined', which is a term of close, but not necessarily sexual, relationship). As Paul implies in 1 Corinthians 6: 16, where he uses the phrase 'becomes one body' to describe the result of sexual intercourse with a prostitute, the physical act on its own does not create an indissoluble union. But sexual unfaithfulness within marriage may be enough to break it.

We are driven to the conclusion that Jesus sanctioned one exception to God's creation ideal. The fact that he did so is a mark of divine mercy towards the frailty of human nature, not a sign that God approves of divorce in some circumstances. But the fact that the exception appears at all, and that it is found on the lips of Jesus, should make all would-be rigorists pause before they insist on too strict a doctrine of the indissolubility of marriage. Human weakness, even among Christians, was not something Jesus dispassionately refused to recognize.

Paul's teaching on divorce

Most of the New Testament's teaching on divorce and re-marriage is concentrated in the four Gospels (the relevant passages, apart from that in Mt. 19, are Mt. 5: 31, 32; Mk. 10: 2–12 and Lk. 16: 18). But in his first letter to the church at Corinth Paul approaches the problem from a fresh angle.

Sexual laxity was rife at Corinth, encouraged by the presence of a thousand prostitute priestesses of Aphrodite who plied their trade openly on the city streets. With this in mind Paul deals with the subject of extra-marital sex in chapter 6 of his letter. Then, in chapter 7, he turns his attention to another problem. No doubt as the result of seeing so much abuse of sex around them, some Christian married couples were opting out of the physical side of married life altogether, in order (as they thought) to become more holy. They are mistaken, says Paul (verses 3–6). A few were even contemplating separation or divorce, and Paul has no hesitation in condemning this course of action too, on the authority of Jesus (verses 10, 11). He does not quote Jesus' exception 'for unchastity', presumably because a reference to extra-marital sex would not have been appropriate at this point. But there was one particularly difficult set of circumstances at Corinth with which Jesus had not dealt explicitly, and on this Paul feels he must give a judgment.

Because Corinth was a mission field, it sometimes happened that one partner in a non-Christian marriage got converted, and occasionally his (or her) new-found faith became a rock of dissent on which the marriage threatened to capsize. What should the Christian do in such a situation? Paul's mind is clear. His apostolic ruling is that the Christian partner should never take the initiative in seeking a divorce, but 'if the unbelieving partner desires to separate, let it be so; in such a case the brother or sister is not bound' (verse 15). The word for 'separate' was often used as a synonym for divorce, and the allusion to bondage strengthens the impression that Paul has full divorce in mind here, not just legal separation (which had no counterpart in the ancient statute-book anyway, although Paul has referred to a kind of *de facto* separation a few sentences earlier).

The really significant thing about this judgment of Paul's is the distinction he draws between the believer and the unbeliever. So long as the unbeliever is prepared to stay, he says, the believer must not even contemplate a divorce. It is only when the unbelieving partner packs his (or her) bags and leaves that the Christian partner is relieved of the responsibility of prolonging the marriage. The assumption is that a Christian has more 'staying-power' in times of marital crisis. If this is true, why should it be so?

Almost certainly, Paul has in the back of his mind the definition of Christian love he expounds so vividly in his letter to the Ephesians. There, in chapter 5, he tells Christian husbands to model their love for their wives on Christ's self-abandoned love for his church (Eph. 5: 25). The Bible has four words for love, but only one of them, the word Paul uses here, is reserved to describe the love of God and its reflection in the lives of Christians. Other kinds of love need some measure of response if they are to flourish, but *agapē*-love survives and even intensifies when it gets no love back in return. A relevant illustration of *agapē's* staying-power appears in Ezekiel's description of God's marriage-covenant with Jerusalem. Ezekiel tells how the 'bride' has flirted promiscuously, and (even by Jesus' standards) deserves to be divorced. 'I will judge you as women who break wedlock,' says God, with perfect justification. But, even so, divine love dictates forgiveness and reconciliation in the end. 'I will remember my covenant with you in the days of your youth . . . when I forgive you all that you have done, says the Lord God' (Ezk. 16).

Just as an 'irresistible temptation' really only means that a particular temptation has not been resisted, 'irretrievable breakdown' tells us more about a husband and wife than it does about their marriage. It tells us that they have given up. The outstanding feature about *agapē*-love is that it never gives up, even when it is thrown back into the teeth of the lover. And it is this special kind of love, on which the believer can draw because he belongs to Christ, that Paul asks his readers to display when their marriages are threatened by imminent breakdown.

This, of course, sets an enormously high standard. To some it may seem impossibly demanding – which is perhaps why Paul adds to his strict demand 'that the (Christian) wife should not separate from her husband' the rather strange proviso *'but if she does*, let her remain single or else be reconciled to her husband' (1 Cor. 7: 10, 11). Like Jesus, Paul was not oblivious to human weakness. Even Christians, with their unique love-potential, can find that marriage poses unbearable problems, and in those circumstances separation may well offer the best practicable solution.

The Bible, then, does not close the door so tightly on divorce and remarriage as some exponents of indissolubility would like. In particular, two situations are described by the New Testament in which divorce is permissible. In the case of sexual unfaithfulness, or in a spiritually mixed marriage when the non-Christian insists on leaving home, the believer is free to accept a divorce and marry again, and any who would deny him that freedom are in danger of being more strict than Jesus and his apostle Paul.

Nevertheless, if the Bible's attitude to divorce is not absolutely rigid, it is extremely rigorous. God's intention for marriage is a lifelong, exclusive union, and anything less is a lapse from the divine ideal. God hates divorce (Mal. 2: 16). Our attention today tends to be riveted by the exceptions Scripture allows, but this was not the impression gained by those who listened to Jesus and his disciples in New Testament times. 'If such is the case of a man with his wife,' gasped the disciples when Jesus had finished his teaching on one occasion, 'it is not expedient to marry' (Mt. 19: 10).

This is not to say that the church must turn its back on those who have made a wreck of married life. As Jesus dealt tenderly with the woman caught red-handed in the act of committing adultery, Christians must show positive compassion and give practical encouragement to those who are trying to rebuild lives broken by divorce. But to pretend that God's marriage standards do not exist – or that they do not matter – is to show a cruel, counterfeit kindness towards a society in which men and women crave the warmth and predictability that only a stable relationship can offer.

Questions for discussion

1. What should be the attitude of Christians, collectively and individually, to those who have been divorced?

2. What circumstances, if any, justify a Christian in seeking a divorce? Do they justify remarriage too?

3. Should divorcees be allowed to remarry in church?

For further reading

J. R. W. Stott, *Divorce* (Falcon, 1972)
J. Murray, *Divorce* (Presbyterian and Reformed, 1961)
A. R. Winnett, *The Church and Divorce* (Mowbray, 1968)

6

5 WORK

'A Christian young lady of fortune', suggests one of George Eliot's characters in *Middlemarch*, 'should find her ideal of life in village charities, patronage of the humbler clergy, the perusal of Female Scripture Characters . . . and the care of her soul over her embroidery in her boudoir – with a background of prospective marriage to a man who – if less strict than herself, as being involved in *affairs religiously inexplicable* – might be prayed for, and seasonably exhorted.'[1]

Middlemarch is, of course, a period piece, set in days long before organized labour and Women's Lib. appeared on the industrial scene, but the description of a Monday-to-Friday job as an 'affair religiously inexplicable' (the italics are mine) is not wholly out of tune with the attitude some Christians adopt towards their daily work. A job is seen simply as the long, dull tunnel that separates Sundays, which are the *Lord's* days when his work can be done. Discussion of major social issues, such as the merits of alternative economic systems or the problems of industrial relations, seems vaguely unspiritual – the kind of thing, in fact, that can thankfully be left to the politicians.

This is admittedly only a caricature. There are many Christians who do see their daily jobs as important outlets for serving God, and an increasing number who are becoming seriously involved in attempts to apply Christian insights to the complex problems posed by a highly industrialized society. Those who secretly regard such efforts as a

[1] G. Eliot, *Middlemarch* (Chatto, 1950).

waste of valuable time which might be spent more profitably in a mid-week church activity may themselves be surprised to discover just how much Scripture has to say about work and working relationships. Conditions of work in Bible times were, of course, very different from those of today, which means that the greatest care must be taken in carrying biblical teaching across the time and culture gap of so many centuries, but there are important basic principles in the Bible which remain relevant to man's working life in this or any other age.

The Bible and work

1. A God who works

The Bible's doctrine of God sets the scene for the very high view of work that Scripture presents. With great daring, the Old Testament writers describe God as a manual labourer, working with his hands and fingers to make the world. He is the Potter, elbow-deep in clay (Is. 45: 9). The whole of creation is 'the work of his hands' (Ps. 8: 3, 6), and, like any worker, he has his rest day (Gn. 2: 2, 3). He even experiences deep job-satisfaction (Gn. 1: 31).

Some religious thinkers in Bible times found the idea of a working God abhorrent. They invented a 'demiurge', a semi-divine clerk of works whose job it was to supervise the messy business of bringing the world into being, so the Supreme Being (as they thought) would not have to dirty his hands with the nuts and bolts of creation. In strong contrast, the Genesis creation account has no room for any demiurge. The God of the Bible is a God who works.

Jesus, too, described his main life-purpose in working terms. Towards the beginning of his ministry, when his disciples urged him to stop for a meal, he replied, 'My food is to do the will of him who sent me, and to accomplish his work' (Jn. 4: 34). And nearing the end of his life he could say to his Father in prayer, 'I glorified thee on earth, having

83

accomplished the work which thou gavest me to do' (Jn. 17: 4).

Jesus' main life-work was, of course, absolutely unique – the work of redemption – but he was also a working man in the more normal, everyday sense. His contemporaries knew him as the carpenter of Nazareth (Mk. 6: 3), and in New Testament times carpentry was a physically demanding trade. There was no works store down the Nazareth High Street to supply a convenient piece of three-by-two on demand. In all probability, a joiner in Jesus' day would have had to cut and fetch his own timber before starting to make a table or chair (without, of course, the aid of power-tools). And it was in this muscle-building trade that Jesus spent all but three years of his working life. The hands which held the whip that drove the crooked money-changers from the temple in Jerusalem had been hardened by years of work with an axe, a saw and a hammer. Tough, physical labour was not beneath the dignity of the Son of God.

2. Working man
Against this backcloth of a working God, it is hardly surprising to find Scripture taking a very high view of the dignity of human labour. The first chapters of Genesis make it quite plain that work was part of God's ideal creation plan for mankind from the very beginning. Adam was instructed to 'till and keep' the Garden of Eden (Gn. 2: 15), a combination of agricultural labour and estate management which must have added up to a most demanding job. Earlier still, the very first command God gave to man included an order to work (Gn. 1: 28), and there is an important sense in which the modern nuclear physicist, the explorer, and the man on the production line are still fulfilling those primeval instructions from the Creator to 'fill the earth and subdue it'. From a Christian point of view, it is by no means naïve to say that God continues his work of sustaining creation today through man's labour. One only has to list the numbers of those involved in the food trade, for example, from the

growing of raw materials in the fields to the packaging of goods and service in the shops, to realize just how much human work is involved in answering the simple prayer, 'Give us this day our daily bread.' This was something the Reformers saw very clearly. 'God even milks the cows through you,' insisted Martin Luther.[2]

It is therefore quite wrong to see work as a side-effect of human sin, something invented by the Devil to ruin man's leisurely enjoyment of God's world. The Bible certainly teaches us that man's fall into sin spoiled working conditions (in Genesis 3, for the first time, we are told that the ground resisted Adam's efforts to work it), but the arrival of sin could do nothing to negate God's creation ideal. Man was created in the image of a working God, and work is as natural to him as sunset is to day (Ps. 104: 19, 23).

In the last book of the Bible, there may even be a hint that the value of the work we do now will not be lost in heaven. Those who 'die in the Lord', we are told, will 'rest from their *labours*' (an umbrella term for all the unpleasant and painful aspects of toil which are a legacy from the Fall), but 'their *works* follow them' (Rev. 14: 13, av). Dr Leon Morris's comments on this verse are worth repeating: 'Heaven is not so much a place where no work is done as one where pain has ceased. The believer rests from his *labours*, but his *works* go into the life beyond the grave. This gives dignity to all the work in which Christian men engage. They are occupied in no insignificant task.'[3] The dream of a workless paradise is clearly not a vision of heaven.

The Bible, then, shows us a working God who has made man to be a worker too. Fitting the pieces together, three practical conclusions emerge.

In the first place, *it is bad for man to refuse work*. This is a conclusion the Bible itself underlines in both Old and New Testaments. 'If anyone will not work,' writes Paul with

[2] Quoted by C. F. H. Henry, *Aspects of Christian Social Ethics* (Eerdmans, 1964), p. 43.
[3] L. Morris, Tyndale Commentary on *Revelation* (IVP, 1969), p. 183.

brutal bluntness, 'let him not eat' (2 Thes. 3: 10). The book of Proverbs is rather more colourful: 'Go to the ant, O sluggard; consider her ways, and be wise' (Pr. 6: 6). Scripture has no time for idlers.

Secondly, on the same grounds, *it must be wrong to deprive a man of work*. Because God intended man to be a worker, to deny any fit person the opportunity of employment is to rob him of something essential to his full humanity. Even social security payments, however generous, are inadequate compensation for enforced unemployment, because the welfare state's charity is no substitute for the contribution God intends a working man to make towards the upkeep and improvement of his society. As William Temple wrote, referring to the unemployed in Jarrow in the slump of the '20s and '30s, 'The gravest and bitterest injury of their state is not the animal grievance of hunger or discomfort, nor even the mental grievance of vacuity and boredom; it is the spiritual grievance of being allowed no opportunity of contributing to the general life and welfare of the community.'[4] Television documentaries on unemployment in Northern Ireland bear striking witness to the truth of Temple's words. The listlessness and sadness on the faces in the dole queue testify to the emptiness of life without work.

Then, thirdly and positively, it follows from this biblical teaching that *work has a very high value*. It is at this point especially that the Christian finds himself in conflict with those whose life-style assumes that work is something inevitably oppressive and burdensome. 'If the daily job is no longer the most time-*consuming* aspect of human existence,' suggested Carl Henry, when editor of the American periodical *Christianity Today*, 'it has nonetheless for countless thousands become life's most time-*oppressive* factor.'[5] The way some advertisements are worded shows that this is no exaggeration. When a job is advertised, it is comparatively

[4] F. A. Iremonger, *William Temple* (OUP, 1948), p. 440.
[5] C. F. H. Henry, *Aspects of Christian Social Ethics*, p. 32.

rarely that any stress is laid on the work involved, especially if this is likely to be strenuous or arduous. The spotlight may fall on the size of the salary (payable at the end of a week's work); the amount of annual holiday (to be taken as a break from work); the extent of sickness benefits (when the applicant is too sick to work); or the size of the pension (to be paid when he is too old to work); on anything, in fact, but the job itself and the work it demands.

Advertisers both reflect and reinforce the spirit of the age, and naturally it is difficult for an individual to resist their pressure. Nevertheless, an attitude of mind which looks upon work as man's supreme indignity (little more than an unfortunately necessary means to a pay-packet or salary-cheque) is clearly out of line with Scripture. The fact that God works, invests all work with dignity. And the fact that he created man to work, invests all work with normality. To look forward longingly to the time when we need work only a one-day week, or put our feet up on the mantelpiece and do no work at all, is not only sub-Christian thinking; according to the Bible, it is sub-*human* too.

Personal attitudes

All that has been said so far threads its way back to the Bible's account of man's creation, as a worker, in the image of the working God. There is an important sense, therefore, in which creation teaching speaks to all men, whether or not they have found faith in Jesus Christ. But there is also a considerable body of biblical teaching which is directed specifically to the Christian, setting out a distinctively Christian approach to work.

1. *Vocation*
First and foremost, according to the Bible, *every Christian has a vocation*. There is a great deal of misunderstanding on this score. Fastened to the wall in the central square of a

well-known theological college are several notice-boards, on which the names of college prize-winners are inscribed in gold lettering. Until recently, one of those boards was reserved for the names of past students who had gone overseas to serve as missionaries. That board has now been removed and taken elsewhere, not because overseas interest in the college has waned, but because it was very wisely recognized that a list of missionaries is out of place in a roll-call of prize-winners. Nevertheless, the attitude to Christian vocation which caused the board to be put there in the first place, still survives in the church.

The tendency to catalogue jobs in some kind of spiritual football league table is deeply engrained on the Christian mind. Way out at the top of the list come those who have 'vocations' – including, no doubt, missionaries and clergy, followed at a short distance by RE teachers, doctors and nurses. Halfway down, we meet those with 'ordinary jobs' (such as businessmen, electrical engineers and secretaries who do not work for Christian organizations). Then, right at the bottom, and in serious danger of relegation, are those involved in much more dubious pursuits – pop musicians, perhaps (unless they subscribe to *Buzz*), and barmaids.

This division of jobs into vocations and 'others' is quite foreign to Scripture. The Bible's approach to work assumes that every man should have a job, and that every Christian, whatever his job, has a vocation. Vocation, after all, only means 'calling'. Indeed, we cramp the style of Scripture cruelly if we confine the meaning of vocation to our weekday employment. Every Christian is called by God to *do* something with his life, and to *be* something for him. When Paul wrote to the church at Ephesus, he was only too well aware that he was addressing a very mixed crowd of converts. In the congregation there were employers and ex-thieves, housewives and children, as well as slaves (which, as we shall see, was a term that covered a broad spectrum of working people). Yet, in spite of this widely-divergent range of occupations, he was able to say to all his readers, 'I therefore, a prisoner for the Lord, beg you to lead a life worthy of the calling to which you have been called' (Eph. 4: 1).

In another of his letters, Paul compares the shameless jostling for key jobs in the church to a state of civil war among the limbs and organs of the body. He points out that it is the smaller and often neglected parts which perform some of the most vital functions (1 Cor. 12). If it is within the spirit of Scripture to extend the force of this teaching to all work – Monday to Friday as well as Sunday – the Christian must beware of falling into the trap of valuing one occupation above another. Using Paul's analogy, to exalt the 'spiritual' work of the missionary over the 'secular' work of the plumber is really to say that the tongue is more important than the kidneys. As far as the Christian is concerned, all jobs can be sacred (when they are done in obedience to God's will), and all are secular (because they are worked out in the world).

Every Christian has a vocation. That much is plain from the Bible. But what is equally clear is that a Christian's vocation cannot be limited artificially to his trade or profession. If it is, then the shortening of the working week becomes something of an embarrassment. How, it may be asked, is a Christian on a three-day week to view his vocation, when he spends more time away from his job than he does doing it?

One answer suggested by an American writer is that he should look for his life's calling in out-of-work activities. That, however, would be a most inadequate solution. To regard one's bread-and-butter job as a mere make-weight results, as we have seen, in a sub-Christian view of work. It might also lead some Christians into a state of frustration and even breakdown, if increasing responsibilities at the office make the idea of a three-day week, in their cases, rather a poor kind of joke. This is a stress that many Christian businessmen experience now. As the pressures at work grow, weekday church activities are either skimped or abandoned, and if out-of-work activities have come to be regarded as the main focus of vocation, it is not hard to imagine what heart-searching and tension may result.

The biblical answer (as is clear from Eph. 4: 1) is that God's calling cannot be tied down to any particular activity. Vocation extends to all hours, as well as to all jobs. The balance between so-called 'working' and 'non-working' hours may differ between individuals; it will probably also vary in the individual's own experience from time to time. But no Christian (providing he is living faithfully) can ever step outside the boundaries of his vocation. So to fret over time spent at an office desk which might have been devoted to a church Bible class may be to misunderstand the all-embracing scope of God's calling.

2. Motivation

Inevitably, if a man is convinced that he has a vocation from God, his motivation for work will be deeply affected, too.

The experts are divided as to exactly what makes people work harder. The profit motive, which might seem to provide the main stimulus, is usually played down nowadays. J. A. C. Brown, for example, writes: 'Without exception, all industrial psychologists are agreed that money is of much less significance than has hitherto been supposed. Except under conditions when wages are very low or during periods of inflation, money is one of the least powerful incentives.'[6] Even with this proviso, the ordinary working man might be allowed an incredulous whistle at that, but it is nevertheless true that other powerful factors, besides money, do influence our approach to work. Prospects of promotion spur some, while the promise of more leisure time attracts others. Even the call of job-satisfaction is not altogether a voice from the past.

For the Christian with a vocation, however, there is one overriding incentive. Above everything else, he does his work to please God. In the New Testament it is Paul who sets out

[6] J. A. C. Brown, *The Social Psychology of Industry* (Penguin, 1954), pp. 201f.

the consequences of this unique source of motivation most clearly. 'Work heartily,' he tells Christian slaves at Colossae, 'as serving the Lord and not men' (Col. 3: 23). After issuing a similar instruction to slaves in the congregation at Ephesus, he amplifies it a little: ' . . . not in the way of eye-service, as men-pleasers, but as servants of Christ, doing the will of God from the heart, rendering service with a good will as to the Lord and not to men' (Eph. 6: 6, 7).

Workers with a sense of vocation are inevitably men and women with ambition. Whole-heartedness demands that no Christian can simply relax as soon as he has mastered his job or collected enough capital to retire comfortably. God's calling drives him to the limits of his physical and mental capacities. 'Oh to be nothing!' can never, therefore, be a Christian's prayer. To be sure, an overwhelming desire to please Christ is quite distinct from any self-seeking incentive, but in practical terms the results may be much the same. In most firms, hard work, however motivated, brings added responsibility, which in turn normally means promotion. One of the reasons (though only one) why so few Christians are to be found in unskilled jobs may well be that Christian commitment stretches capabilities and opens up new horizons. As Carl Henry provocatively observes, 'to turn a screw with Job-like patience on an assembly line is no reproach if it represents one's highest level of creative ability. Such limitation is sinful, however, for a disciple of Christ who has greater potential for service.'[7]

Mention of work on an assembly line, however, raises one powerful objection. Modern working conditions are patently very different from those of Bible times. A Ford welfare-worker tells of a revealing conversation he once had with a man on the assembly line in a Detroit factory:

'What are you making?' he asked.
'C429,' came the bored reply.
'What is C429?'

[7] C. F. H. Henry, *Aspects of Christian Social Ethics*, p. 61.

'I don't know.'
'What becomes of C429 when it leaves you?'
'I don't know.'
'How long have you been making C429?'
'Nine years.'[8]

Is it not simply naïve, he asked, looking back on this exchange, to demand of anyone – even the most ardent Christian – that he should spend nine whole-hearted years making a C429? Even a slave in Bible times could work creatively; he was at least near enough to the finished product to be able to take a pride in his job. But standing in front of a machine that stamps out brackets for forty-two hours a week can hardly be called 'creative' by any stretch of the imagination.

Hard though it may be, this is an objection the Christian is bound to resist. If he is on the management side, of course, he has a responsibility to relieve the boredom of others and to heighten their job-satisfaction.[9] But even if he is powerless to make changes, uncongenial conditions cannot rob the Christian worker of his unique incentive. Paul's all-embracing command to 'work heartily' was written to slaves, and anyone who imagines that a slave at Colossae was the ancient counterpart of a mellow eighteenth-century English craftsman should have his rose-tinted spectacles removed. Not every slave-master was kind and gentle (cf. 1 Pet. 2: 18). Most regarded their slave-labour as just another part of the over-all plant, which an efficient employer would renew at regular intervals. One Roman farming handbook [1] divided agricultural implements into three categories – the 'mute' (meaning the farm vehicles), the 'inarticulate' (the animals), and the 'articulate' (the slaves); and it was the author's advice that a new man just taking over an estate should make it his very first job to go round and throw out all the ineffi-

[8] Quoted by S. Cave, *The Christian Way* (Nisbet, 1949), p. 207.
[9] For the responsibilities of management, see further on pp. 98ff.
[1] Varro (116–27 BC), *De Re Rustica*.

cient tools in each category – mute or articulate. When to this is added the fact that most white- and blue-collar workers were slaves in New Testament times (including doctors, teachers and accountants), Paul's instructions become all the more remarkable.

All too often the slave's working conditions were far from congenial, and he had no security against instant redundancy. Nor is the contrast between creative work and routine monotony one that we find stressed in Scripture. If anything, the Bible views so-called 'creative' work with some suspicion, because admiration of 'the work of men's hands' could so easily lead to idolatry (*cf.* Ps. 115: 4; Is. 40: 19). On balance, therefore, the Christian is not entitled to plead, 'Give me the right conditions – *then* I will work whole-heartedly.'

Social issues

If conditions of work were frequently oppressive, it is puzzling to find so little criticism in the New Testament of the social environment in which slavery flourished. Why did Paul content himself with giving advice to masters and slaves on the way they should behave towards one another, when instead he might have aimed a broadside against the institution of slavery itself? The Bible disappoints many radicals by its apparently kid-gloved approach to the corrupt institutions of society. Jesus, say his critics, did not go nearly far enough in his fight for social justice. He had a great many compassionate things to say to the deprived and downtrodden. He also had some sharp words for the representatives of the selfish rich, and for members of the hypocritical religious establishment. But he *did* virtually nothing to change the social environment in which all the unfairness and suffering flourished.

The criticism has spilled over into modern times. Professor Tawney, for example, scorning the church's timidity in soft-pedalling the problems of industrial conflict, con-

93

cludes that Christians 'relieved the wounded and comforted the dying but they dared not enter the battle'.[2]

Brian Wren tells a modern parable with the same message.[3] 'There was once a factory which employed thousands of people. Its production line was a miracle of modern engineering, turning out thousands of machines every day. The factory had a high accident rate. The complicated machinery of the production line took little account of human error, forgetfulness or ignorance. Day after day, men came out of the factory with squashed fingers, cuts, bruises. Sometimes a man would lose an arm or a leg. Occasionally someone was electrocuted or crushed to death.

'Enlightened people began to see that something needed to be done. First on the scene were the churches. An enterprising minister organized a small first-aid tent outside the factory gate. Soon, with the backing of the Council of Churches, it grew into a properly-built clinic, able to give first-aid to quite serious cases, and to treat minor injuries. The town council became interested, together with local bodies like the Chamber of Trade and the Rotary Club. The clinic grew into a small hospital, with modern equipment, an operating theatre, and a full-time staff of doctors and nurses. Several lives were saved. Finally, the factory management, seeing the good that was being done, and wishing to prove itself enlightened, gave the hospital its official backing, with unrestricted access to the factory, a small annual grant, and an ambulance to speed serious cases from workshop to hospital ward.

'But, year by year, as production increased, the accident rate continued to rise. More and more people were hurt or maimed. And, in spite of everything the hospital could do, more and more people died from the injuries they had received. Only then did some people begin to ask if it was

[2] Quoted by H. F. R. Catherwood, *The Christian in Industrial Society* (IVP, 1964), p. 29.

[3] B. Wren, *A Modern Parable* (published by the Churches' Action for World Development).

94

enough to treat people's injuries, while leaving untouched the machinery that caused them.'

While taking Brian Wren's point, it is not, of course, by any means accurate to say that the church has shown no interest in promoting social reforms. It was Christians who spearheaded the fight for the abolition of slavery in Britain in the nineteenth century. In defence of the Bible's comparative silence on this particular issue, it could also be pointed out that the harsh realities of political life in New Testament times blocked the outlets for social agitation that are open to Christians now. With few exceptions, the first disciples were men and women drawn from the lower ranks of society. Living under a totalitarian regime, they had no political influence to wield. They could do nothing of a practical nature to rectify the social evils of their day. The seeds of social change were certainly sown in the New Testament's demand for equality between master and slave *in the church* (*cf.* Gal. 3: 28), but it would be unfair to reproach these early Christians for failing to take political action.

Working relationships

Nevertheless, such criticisms of Christ and the church do serve to highlight the fact that Jesus' approach to social issues differed in important respects from that of some would-be reformers today. He saw the root of social evil in people rather than in institutions. Being a true radical himself, therefore, his method was to work through individuals into society, rather than vice versa. So, for example, we find him dealing with Zacchaeus, the crooked tax-collector of Jericho, instead of issuing a general manifesto denouncing financial corruption in high places (Lk. 19: 2 ff.). Above all, Jesus sought to bring individual men and women into full personal commitment to God, knowing that genuine faith would have far-reaching social consequences.

Some modern industrial commentators are also stressing

95

the personal factor in dealing with problems of work and economics. For example, Sir Frederick Catherwood, when Director General of the National Economic Development Council, wrote: 'The problems of this age are not technical ... If you look at the economy of any country and you begin to probe the reasons for slow progress; if you try to find why personal income instead of rising at 10 per cent per annum rises only at 4 or 2 per cent or not at all, then you very quickly discover that the reasons are not technical but human.'[4] The title of the 1971 Industrial *Relations* Act (now repealed) was itself a tacit admission that at the root of industrial conflicts lie bad relationships. Naturally, the improving of working relationships will penetrate to changes in structures. The two inevitably intermesh. But the starting-point is all-important. Should the focus be on organizations and structures – or on relationships and people?

The Bible tells us that one major result of man's fall into sin was the spoiling of working relationships, dating right back to the row between Abel the herdsman and Cain the arable farmer recorded for us in Genesis 4. And the later laws of the Old Testament reflect two areas particularly in which sin ruins relationships – now as then.

1. Seller and buyer

The Bible has some harsh words for tradesmen who cheat their customers: 'You shall not have in your bag two kinds of weights, a large and a small. You shall not have in your house two kinds of measures, a large and a small ... For all who do such things, all who act dishonestly, are an abomination to the Lord your God' (Dt. 25: 13, 14, 16). Micah tells how 'the voice of the Lord cries to the city . . . "Shall I acquit the man with wicked scales and with a bag of deceitful weights?"' (Mi. 6: 9, 11).

Although Her Majesty's Inspector of Weights and Measures have dealt a blow to those who weight their scales and give short measure from their petrol pumps, the cheat is still

[4] H. F. R. Catherwood, *The Christian Citizen* (Hodder, 1970), p. 36.

alive and well in the High Streets of the twentieth century. There are more sophisticated ways today of pulling wool over the consumer's eyes. Misleading guarantees lull the customer into a false sense of security. Inflated 'recommended prices' deceive the housewife into thinking she is getting fantastic bargains when in fact she is only helping to swell already bloated profit margins; and unrealistic delivery dates add to the frustration and disillusionment. If the Old Testament prophets were alive today, they might want to change a few of their illustrations, but their underlying message would still keep its contemporary bite.

More than any other area of business life, one suspects that modern advertising would provide a twentieth-century prophet with a ready-made target. Given an economic system based on competition, some persuasive kind of advertising is inevitable. The producer cannot rest content merely with informing the public of his product's existence. He must do his best to convince those on the other side of the printed page or television screen that his wares are superior to all other brands (even though the 'competing' firms may be members of the same consortium). Inevitably, too, advertisements mirror the standards that already prevail in society. Unpleasant traits in human nature, such as pride, avarice and desire for self-gratification, are harnessed in the seller's interests, and this is a trend that leaves the Christian particularly uneasy. No-one can pretend, of course, that the advertiser actually creates greed, but it is difficult to avoid the conclusion that, in stimulating avarice by the most persuasive means at his disposal, he is strengthening the grip of something the Christian is dedicated to destroy.

It is arguable, too, that the advertiser's tendency to treat the potential customer as a mere unit in profit-making comes very close to the unscrupulous approach to selling which Scripture condemns. Although subliminal advertising is banned by law in the United Kingdom, and it would be an exaggeration to claim that a trip down a London Underground escalator represents the first stage in brain-washing, it is enough to set the alarm bells ringing to discover that some agencies employ professional psychologists to identify and stimulate the consumer's irrational urges. Despite the highly commendable standards demanded by bodies such as the Independent Broadcasting Authority and the Advertising Standards Authority, and the safeguards of the Trade Descriptions Act, modern advertising is still a dangerous weapon in the hands of those with few moral scruples.

2. Employer and employee

As well as spoiling the proper relationship of honesty and trust that should exist between seller and buyer, sin also drives a deep wedge between the worker and those who employ him.

In the power-structures of the biblical world, the boss held all the cards, and Scripture is particularly sharp in condemning employers who used their powers to exploit their labour force. 'Woe to him who builds his house by unrighteousness, and his upper rooms by injustice,' thunders Jeremiah; 'who makes his neighbour serve him for nothing, and does not give him his wages' (Je. 22: 13). And in the New Testament we find James sounding the same warning: 'Behold, the wages of the labourers who mowed your fields, which you kept back by fraud, cry out; and the cries of the harvesters have reached the ears of the Lord of hosts' (Jas. 5: 4). In face of verses like these, it is curious to find the Marxist still criticizing Christianity as 'the opiate of the masses'.

The sad story of industrial relations in Britain underlines the fact that the selfish, greedy employer has by no means vanished from the modern scene. The drive to maximize profits and improve efficiency means that in some sectors of industry commercial considerations have been allowed to override the human interests of employees, and as Kuyper reminds us, 'to mistreat the workman as "a piece of machinery" is and remains a violation of his human dignity. Even worse, it is a sin going squarely against the sixth command-

98

ment, thou shalt not kill.'[5] Ultimately, the gap between humane treatment and efficient productivity may not be nearly so wide as is sometimes imagined. Vehicle producers in France and Italy, for example, are finding that productivity improves once workers are allowed the satisfaction of building a whole car, instead of fixing a single component on a conveyor belt. But there will always be a tendency, especially in the short term, to treat people as tools in the interests of maximum profit, and this is something that has to be strongly resisted on Christian grounds. Very often it is those in middle management who find themselves cast as the villains of the piece. In order not to become victims themselves (and it is no laughing matter to be put out of a job in one's fifties), they feel forced to comply with the constant demands for ever-expanding profit-margins droned out from faraway head offices.

It is here that the Trade Unions have a particularly important role to fulfil. Much middle-class Christian prejudice against the Unions is born out of misunderstanding. The principle of corporate solidarity which arms any group of workers with bargaining power is deeply engrained in Scripture. So, too, is the principle of social justice which the TUC exists to defend. Time and time again in the Bible we are told how God is specially concerned to see that the weak receive just treatment (see, for example, Is. 1: 17; 58: 6 ff.; Am. 5: 10 ff.); and there is little doubt that the individual worker would still find himself both weak and oppressed if he were deprived of his right to associate. The Trade Union movement also anticipated the welfare state in providing for such things as sickness benefits and funeral grants. It was not for nothing that shop stewards earned their nickname 'the parsons of industry'.

This is not to pretend, of course, that employers have a monopoly on sin. Employees can be selfish and greedy too. In his parable of the workers in the vineyard, Jesus drew attention to the dog-in-the-manger attitude of those who

[5] A. Kuyper, *Christianity and the Class Struggle* (Piet Hein, 1950), p.57.

resent generous treatment offered to others and insist on leap-frogging their wage-rises (Mt. 20: 13 ff.). He also taught that 'the labourer deserves his wages' (Lk. 10: 7); but he would not have disagreed with John the Baptist's warning to the professional soldiers who came to him for baptism: 'Rob no one by violence or by false accusation, and be content with your wages' (Lk. 3: 14). Soldiers in New Testament times were powerful men; they could boost their wage-packets with the aid of threats. Their modern counterparts, perhaps, are those organized bodies of workers who are aware that they control the key areas of industry and are tempted to use their strength to hold others to ransom. A cry for 'fair shares' may be little more than a cloak for greed. In the Old Testament, the principle of corporate solidarity is seen mostly in *national* terms. If this principle were to be applied strictly today, it would presumably mean that employers and employees should sink their differences in working together for the good of the whole body politic.

It is in the light of biblical teaching such as this that the rights and wrongs of *strike action* must be weighed. In 1961, Archbishop Fisher wrote, 'I think it is an unrighteous thing ever to strike for money, except possibly when you are starving.'[6] Many strikes, of course, are not about money at all. But even if we restrict the field to disputes over pay, it is by no means clear that strike action must always be ruled out as immoral on Christian grounds. If an employer is justified in withholding his goods from sale when he feels the price offered is not a fair one, the demands of justice make it difficult to condemn an employee who withholds his labour when he fails to get the proper market value for it. It would be hard to disagree with Joseph Hume's judgment in a parliamentary speech of the last century: 'Labour is the commodity of men, as capital is of the masters, and both are allowed to obtain the best terms they can.'

At the same time, many strikes are blatantly selfish and unjustified. Sometimes they reflect impatience with slow-

[6] In a *Daily Herald* article, 26 November 1961.

moving negotiating machinery. The Shop Stewards Handbook of one major union, for example, warns against over-hasty reactions in a time of dispute. All the relevant facts must be collected, weighed and carefully considered before any action is taken.[7] Yet on many occasions men belonging to this Union have chosen to take unofficial action rather than go through the set procedures of arbitration. A call for solidarity may mask a very selfish and impatient kind of collective greed. The protests of Union officials, that they have no wish to make others suffer through a strike, often have a particularly hollow ring about them.

The Bible upholds the principle of corporate concern, but it condemns the kind of solidarity which has no interest or compassion for those outside the immediate group. Jesus himself told the parable of the Good Samaritan to point out the inadequacy of too narrow a concept of neighbourliness. That is why a just cause will not automatically bring a Christian out on strike. He must first calculate the consequences of his action on others – from the men who will be laid off in a factory fifty miles away, to the underprivileged in other countries who may be paid less for the raw materials they supply – and then weigh these against the size and urgency of his own grievance. In nature, a bird builds its own nest but is not responsible for seeing that all other birds have nests as well. A very similar law of the jungle applies all too often in industrial life, but the Christian cannot be satisfied with anything less than the all-embracing neighbour-love that Jesus demanded.

So much more could be (and has been) written about the causes and cures of industrial problems, but perhaps enough has been said to illustrate the Bible's wisdom in setting its teaching about work firmly in a context of relationships. Working conditions today may be far from ideal. Large groups of people are employed in vast concerns where personal contact with the employer is out of the question.

[7] The TGWU Shop Stewards Handbook.

Directors share their interests over dozens of companies, while many thousands of workers never set eyes on the finished products they are helping to produce. It all seems a far cry from New Testament times. Yet it could be argued with some force that the conditions of work in Paul's day, under a none-too-benevolent system of slavery, were even worse. His instructions to employers and workers at Ephesus and Colossae must have sounded as ludicrously naïve then as they do now. But he and his readers shared something which gave them the potential to revolutionize all working relationships. And that 'something' was their common faith in a God who is himself a worker.

Questions for discussion

1. Do you agree with the statement on p. 93 that the Christian is not entitled to plead 'Give me the right conditions – *then* I will work whole-heartedly'?

2. Should a Christian be prepared to accept lower standards at work than he would in his private life, as an unfortunate but necessary compromise with the need to live in today's world?

3. 'If he finds himself in a minority, the democratic principle demands that a Christian should sink his personal scruples and join in a strike of which he disapproves.' Do you agree?

For further reading

A. Richardson, *The Biblical Doctrine of Work* (SCM, 1963)
H. F. R. Catherwood, *The Christian in Industrial Society* (IVP, 1964)
M. Ivens (ed.), *Industry and Values* (Harrap, 1970)

6 RACE AND COLOUR

A student and his wife made their way along a street in North London. As they walked, they held hands. There was nothing remarkable about the scene; nothing, in fact, to provoke the deliberate attempt by a woman (whom neither of them knew) to push the girl under the wheels of a passing bus. But these two young people were not altogether unprepared for such an emergency. Her skin was pink, while his was black, and their attempts to find accommodation had already conditioned them to expect suspicion and hostility. Flats which were advertised as vacant when *she* made the initial approach were miraculously withdrawn from the market as soon as *he* arrived on the scene. It was all very mysterious, especially as he, despite the colour of his skin, was an Englishman, Liverpool born and bred.

Colour prejudice is just one of racialism's many ugly heads, but it is the one with which we are most familiar in the western world. Black Power in America, apartheid policies in South Africa, and Powellism with its predictions that 'rivers of blood' will flow if immigration into Britain is not stopped, are all, in their different ways, symptoms of the uneasiness and mistrust which spoil life in racially mixed communities.

Proposals for improving community relations come thick and fast, ranging from suggestions that compulsory segregation should be enforced (because people who fight are best kept apart), to calls for compulsory integration (because only by being forced to live together will their hostility disappear).

And amid all the turmoil of manifestos and counter-demonstrations, churchmen are seen to take different sides. The Archbishop of Canterbury gets wide press coverage for denouncing Enoch Powell's racial fulminations, while a Baptist minister writes an article in *The Christian* under the heading 'We need a theological Enoch Powell'.[1] Martin Luther King dies a martyr's death in the cause of American racial integration, but is outlived by preachers from the deep south such as Charles Conley Lynch, who bases his segregationist views on the belief that 'there is no other book that presents more violence in defence of racial purity' than the Bible.[2] It is all very confusing.

Perhaps most embarrassing of all, from a Christian point of view, is the wide divergence of opinion among church leaders in South Africa on the apartheid issue. As the number of Anglican clergy deported for criticizing the government's racial policies swells, leaders of the Dutch Reformed Church maintain their firm stand on the value and necessity of segregation. Judging from the literature that is available, Christians outside South Africa are generally better acquainted with the case against apartheid than with the arguments in its favour. It may be helpful, therefore, before embarking on a more general discussion of the issues raised by race and colour, to set out the main pro-apartheid arguments in a little more detail – if only because they are heard so seldom. At the very least, those who live in the grimy glasshouses of societies which show little signs of solving their own race problems should take special care before throwing stones at others.

A case for apartheid

The Dutch Reformed Church has its roots in a deep respect

[1] Humphrey Vellacott, in *The Christian*, 24 May 1968.
[2] Quoted in C. Salley and R. Behm, *Your God is too White* (Lion Publishing, 1973), p. 96.

for biblical teaching (a position the South African wing has maintained rather more faithfully than the mother-church in Holland), and there are thousands of sincere Christian Afrikaners who are convinced that the principle of racial segregation accurately mirrors the doctrines of Scripture. Their case for apartheid may be summed up under four headings.

1. Racial diversity is part of God's plan

In his evangelistic address in Athens, Paul appears to make this point very clearly. The Creator God, he says, 'made from one every nation of men to live on the face of the earth, *having determined allotted periods and the boundaries of their habitation*' (Acts 17: 26). In other words, the same God who made the whole of humanity from a common origin (so that no-one can claim 'I am descended from a more distinguished Adam than you', as an adaptation of the Talmud quaintly puts it[3]), divides history and fixes territorial boundaries. There appears to be no inevitable conflict, therefore, between the separating of races and the basic unity of mankind in God's creation plan. When, after the Flood, a group of immigrants attempted to build on a unity which cut across human divisions, the Lord's response was not to applaud their efforts but to confuse their common language as he 'scattered them abroad . . . over the face of all the earth' (Gn. 11: 6–9). The Babel experiment was clearly not in line with the Creator's will.

All over the world, the Afrikaner points out, as people jet their way further and further from home, man's natural instinct to preserve his racial and cultural identity rises to the surface. Holidaymakers travel abroad in groups, so that even in a foreign land they can mix with people who dress their way, eat their kind of food and speak their own language. Travelling businessmen found clubs in foreign cities, so they can relax in congenial company in a home-from-

[3] Quoted in E. Fuller, *Affirmation of God and Man* (Association Press, 1967), pp. 48f.

105

home atmosphere. Even the spiritual needs of ex-patriates are met by special chaplaincy churches so those who find themselves away from home territory on a Sunday can worship in a building that looks like a 'proper' church and has a familiar order of service.

Some may laugh at all this as yet another indication of the human herd instinct. Others may frown on it as a symptom of an unhealthy ghetto mentality. The fact remains that it answers to something very deep in human nature. If people are not forced to live segregated lives, the chances are that they will choose to do so voluntarily.

'In thousands of miles of travel by road and in time spent in all the major cities,' wrote Leslie Lyall, 'I could not help observing how the races everywhere quite happily gravitate to their own society.' 'It is a pity', he write, 'that the Afrikaans word for separateness has become an abusive word to use against South Africa, because separate and equal development is precisely what black people everywhere most desire – in North America, in Britain, or in Africa. Neither the white nor the black races really want integration, and it is just as mistaken to legislate for integration as it is for separation (*apartheid*).'[4]

2. *Apartheid expresses neighbour-love*

As Leslie Lyall hints, and the Dutch Reformed Church vigorously maintains, there is a world of difference in theory between a policy of separate development (*apartheid*) and the idea of white domination (*baaskap*). In spite of all the popular caricatures, segregation does not have to mean that one group of people is treated less favourably than another. Apartheid means 'separate but equal', not 'separate and superior'. In other words, it is possible, at least in theory, to *segregate* races without *discriminating* between them.

Inevitably, as the Christian Afrikaner would admit, there

---

[4] L. T. Lyall, 'Understanding South Africa', in *The Life of Faith*, 14 November 1970. Mr Lyall is referring, of course, to voluntary separation, not to the enforced segregation of South African apartheid law.

are prejudiced white people in South Africa (as there are everywhere else) who use the provisions of the segregation law to exploit non-whites, but it is no more defensible to condemn apartheid by pointing the finger at those who abuse it, than it is to write off the whole of Christianity when one clergyman is found guilty of misconduct. John Vorster, Prime Minister of South Africa, makes it quite clear that apartheid is not a synonym for white domination and oppression, at any rate as far as he is concerned. 'I believe in the policy of separate development,' he writes, 'not only as a philosophy but also as the only practical solution in the interest of everyone to eliminate frictions, and to do justice to every population group as well as every individual. I say to the Coloured people, as well as to the Indians and the Bantu, that the policy of separate development is not a policy which rests upon jealousy, fear or hatred. It is not a denial of the human dignity of anyone nor is it so intended.'[5]

Plenty of evidence can be brought in to support the South African government's claim that it offers non-whites a far better deal in material terms, than they could hope to get anywhere else. Although African workers earn low wages, the fringe benefits they enjoy in education and medical care are enough to convince outside observers, such as the evangelical publisher Gervase Duffield, that the Afrikaners are sincere in the concern they express to improve the living conditions of their Bantu neighbours. 'I did not find an evil racist regime persecuting and suppressing the Bantu,' writes Duffield in a *Crusade* article; 'I found a white Government that had used white tax-payers' money with great generosity towards the Bantu. The South African Government has a fine record of clearing shanty towns and building new black townships . . . I visited a mission hospital which Government money had transformed into a major and well-equipped modern hospital, solely for the benefit of the Bantu in the area . . . I visited the Transkei, and again saw Govern-

[5] In *Progress through Separate Development* (1968), obtainable from the South African Embassy.

ment money being poured into that place, and a number of devoted civil servants, white men and Christians from the Dutch Reformed Church, working under Bantu leadership to develop Bantustans.'[6]

White South Africans would also argue that apartheid benefits the non-white community culturally as well as materially. Indeed, they would say, a firm policy of segregation provides the only realistic protection for Bantu culture, if it is to resist western European influences. In other parts of Africa missionaries have discovered (sometimes too late) that the westernized Christianity they have imported smacks so strongly of European colonialism that the white man's religion has eventually been rejected on political grounds, along with his paternalism. Even in countries such as Britain, where people of different races are encouraged to worship side by side, immigrants tend to band together to form their own congregations, so they can worship in their own idiom. Spiritually and culturally, therefore (the argument goes), segregation seems to be in everyone's best interests. As Dr Malan, ex-premier of South Africa, succinctly puts it in his autobiography, 'Apartheid is based on what the Afrikaner believes to be his divine calling and privilege – to convert the heathen to Christianity without obliterating his national identity.'[7]

3. Racial purity is a biblical principle

Dr Malan faithfully reflects the way the first Christian Afrikaners identified themselves with Old Testament Israel – God's people living among foreigners who shared neither their culture nor their faith. Just as the Israelites were commanded to keep themselves separate from the people of Canaan in Old Testament times, so the pioneer Afrikaner believed he must at all costs retain his separate identity from the coloured people around him, if he was eventually to

[6] G. E. Duffield, in *Crusade*, May 1973, p. 26.
[7] D. F. Malan, *Apartheid: South Africa's Answer to a Major Problem* (Pretoria, 1954).

become a blessing to them. 'The difference in colour', writes Malan, 'is merely a physical manifestation of the contrast between two irreconcilable ways of life, between barbarism and civilization, between heathenism and Christianity.'[8]

The Old Testament vividly shows how God's people courted disaster when they mixed with foreigners, and in no department of life was the standard of separation so rigorously enforced then as it was in the affairs of the heart and family. Intermarriage with those outside the covenant was strictly forbidden – so much so that Nehemiah was provoked to take extreme action when he discovered that some Jews from the newly rebuilt city of Jerusalem were marrying foreign girls. 'I argued with them', he recalls, 'and reviled them, I beat them and tore out their hair; and I made them swear in the name of God: "We will not marry our daughters to their sons, or take any of their daughters in marriage for our sons or for ourselves" ' (Ne. 13: 25, NEB). In the face of rough justice like that, meted out in the cause of maintaining racial purity, the provisions of the South African Immorality Act seem relatively tame!

4. The Bible justifies concessions to human weakness

As we have seen in a previous chapter, Jesus, when he provided for divorce in certain well-defined cases of marriage breakdown, was only following the law of Moses in making concessions to the weakness of human nature. He tempered God's ideal plan for marriage, which had no room for the possibility of divorce at all, to allow for the devastating intrusion of sin on this closest of human relationships. Today, even those churches which believe that the only way to protect marriage is to rule out divorce altogether, do not normally object to the principle of legal separation. If two married people cannot live together without bitterness and cruelty, they must be forced to live apart.

Supporters of apartheid see racial segregation as a natural extension of the same principle. Human weakness demands

[8] *Ibid.*

109

that different racial groups must live apart, if they are to live at peace. The experience of other African nations, where independence has led to the flaring up of ancient tribal feuds, only serves to highlight the wisdom of the Afrikaner's apartheid policy. If the government of South Africa revoked its segregationist principles in favour of majority rule, claims the white South African, the result would be anarchy, not integration; a fierce, bloody conflict for power between three rival racial groups who at present live at peace – because they live apart.

If it is objected that this is a far from ideal solution to the problems of pent-up racial bitterness and tension, many segregationists would agree. But it is better, they would point out, to stay in the frying pan of apartheid than to jump into the fire of racial conflict. We have to accept the world as we find it, resisting wild claims that it can be changed overnight by a wave of the idealist's magic wand. And in making such realistic allowances for the weaknesses of human nature, the Christian can quote Jesus as his example.

From a Christian point of view, it is important to examine the case for apartheid in some detail, not only because it is seldom heard, but because among its strongest supporters it numbers Christians who claim to have tested their attitudes and opinions by the standards of Scripture. There are, of course, many questions that cry out for an answer. If God really intended the boundaries which fence off nations to be inviolable, why does the Bible say that tribal and national migrations find a place in his plan (*e.g.* Am. 9: 7)? If interracial marriages are altogether wrong, why could Moses marry an Ethiopian, and Boaz a Moabitess, apparently with God's approval? And if Christians are not intended to strive after God's ideals in this world now, rather than passively accept an imperfect *status quo*, how can they continue to pray 'Thy will be done, on earth as it is in heaven'? Above all, on what theological grounds can the Afrikaner properly identify his role with that of Israel under the Old Testament

110

theocracy, and how can the Bantu possibly be called 'better off' when their mobility and freedom to make relationships are so tightly restricted?

These questions raise issues no Christian dare sidestep. Nevertheless, to see them in perspective (and raise other issues about race relationships outside South Africa), it will be helpful to view them all against the broader backcloth of the Bible's teaching on the creation and redemption of mankind as a whole. There are, in particular, three areas of biblical doctrine that are outstandingly relevant to any Christian discussion of colour and race.

Biblical principles

1. The creation of man

The Bible's account of man's creation makes it quite clear that there can be no such thing as a superior race in God's sight. Generically, the whole of mankind was created in God's image (Gn. 1: 26, 27; 5: 1; 9: 6; Jas. 3: 9), without racial or cultural distinction. The God of creation shows no partiality in the way he deals with men of different races, as Peter discovered to his astonishment when a vision from God shattered his strictly Jewish racial prejudices. 'Truly', he gasped, 'I perceive that God shows no partiality, but in every nation any one who fears him and does what is right is acceptable to him' (Acts 10: 34).

At first glance, it does seem very much as though the Old Testament's picture of a 'chosen people', with whom God has a special covenant relationship, is a clear case of racial discrimination. Closer examination, however, shows that this is not so at all. Israel was not picked out for any special racial merit (Dt. 7: 7 ff.). Membership of God's people was open to all comers on the same terms, and the non-Jewish sojourner was protected by special legislation. 'When a stranger sojourns with you in your land,' said the covenant law, 'you shall not do him wrong. The stranger who

111

sojourns with you shall be to you as the native among you, and you shall love him as yourself' (Lv. 19: 33, 34). To be accepted as a member of the chosen people, a man did not have to show his birth certificate, but he did have to prove himself willing to worship Israel's God, and to regulate his life by the law of the Lord. The only kind of discrimination we meet in the Old Testament is religious, not racial.

This principle helps to explain the otherwise puzzling prohibitions of inter-racial marriage in the Old Testament, with the exceptions made in the cases of Moses (despite Aaron's opposition to the match – Nu. 12: 9) and Ruth (whose grandson, David, was to be the forbear of Jesus). The reason behind Nehemiah's strong objection to the presence of foreign brides in Jerusalem was not that they had introduced a strange dialect and new habits, but because, along with their foreign customs, they were importing the worship of foreign *gods* (Ne. 13: 26; *cf.* 1 Ki. 11: 1 ff.). The law of Deuteronomy made it perfectly clear why such marriages were forbidden: 'You shall not make marriages with them,' God had decreed, 'giving your daughters to their sons or taking their daughters for your sons. For they would turn away your sons from following me, to serve *other gods*' (Dt. 7: 3, 4).

There is no ban on inter-racial marriage as such in the Old Testament, but there are the strongest possible sanctions against inter-religious unions, and this is a theme which finds an echo in the New Testament too. A Christian, writes Paul, as a member of God's new covenant people, is free to marry anyone he likes – '*only in the Lord*' (1 Cor. 7: 39). Over and above considerations of physical, mental and cultural compatibility, a Christian must choose a life-partner who is a good match spiritually. Does he (or she) trust and serve the same Lord? That is the key question. Obviously there are other questions, too, which must be answered satisfactorily if an inter-racial union is going to be a success, but this biblical teaching is a far cry from the purely racial provisions of the South African Immorality Act, with its ban on all

112

mixed marriages. On grounds of religious compatibility alone, a white English girl might well be justified in turning down an Englishman in favour of a black Ugandan. Many immigrants arrive in Britain with a far more lively Christian faith than they find among the majority of the native residents.

The dignity and equality which creation in the divine image gives to each human being brands every attempt to discriminate between men on racial grounds as abhorrent to God. The Bible tells us how the Lord himself champions those whose basic human rights are ignored. 'He who oppresses a poor man', says the book of Proverbs, in typically blunt fashion, 'insults his Maker' (Pr. 14: 31; *cf.* 17: 5). Translated into modern terms, the denial of any man's equal worth amounts to a slap in God's face. Mark Twain's 'Aunt Sally' is fortunately only a fictional character, but her reaction when Huck Finn reports an accident vividly portrays the kind of racist thinking the Bible condemns as insulting to the Creator:

'Good gracious,' she exclaims. 'Anybody hurt?'

'No'm.,' Huck replied — and then, as an afterthought, 'Killed a nigger.'

'Well, it's lucky, because sometimes people do get hurt.'[9]

Inasmuch as Twain was parodying the attitudes of some white, church-going, text-quoting Christians from the southern States, one can fully understand Malcolm X's hostile reaction when he wrote in his autobiography: 'Christianity is the white man's religion. The Holy Bible in the white man's hands and his interpretations of it have been the greatest single ideological weapon for enslaving millions of non-white human beings.'[1]

Dehumanizing prejudices can show themselves in more subtle ways too. The attitude of mind which reluctantly supports controlled immigration because it supplies necessary labour for unpopular jobs (who else would run the London

[9] Quoted by D. Bronnert, *Race* (Falcon, 1973), p. 3.
[1] Malcolm X, *Autobiography* (Grove Press, 1965), p. 241.

Underground if all the coloureds pulled out?) comes very close to the heresy of treating people as tools. When the 1971 Immigration Bill was published, the Community and Race Relations Unit of the British Council of Churches very properly condemned what it called 'a narrowly conceived idea of British society, in which those of a different colour and culture are tolerated for the services they can render but not welcome for the enrichment they can bring'.[2]

A superior, patronizing attitude to people of other races can even creep into much-respected reference books. Joyce Gladwell, a West Indian graduate of mixed parentage, tells how she felt 'wordless and numb inside' when she read in the school library's copy of *The Encyclopaedia Britannica:* 'The negro in certain . . . characteristics . . . would appear to stand on a lower evolutionary plane than the white man, and to be more closely related to the highest anthropoids . . . The mental constitution of the negro is very similar to that of a child, normally good-natured and cheerful, but subject to sudden fits of emotion and passion during which he is capable of performing acts of singular atrocity, impressionable, vain, but often exhibiting in the capacity of servant a dog-like fidelity which has stood the supreme test.'[3] One wonders whether the compilers of this (the 11th) edition of the famous encyclopaedia had ever read the ancient writer Cicero's estimate of the Celts of Britain as 'exceptionally stupid and unteachable'. Research sponsored by UNESCO shows how the 'Sambo' image of the American negro as a docile, lazy, irresponsible creature is a product of discrimination, not a natural feature of dark-skinned people. Exactly the same psychological symptoms showed themselves in otherwise normal British and American survivors from the Nazi concentration camps of the second world war.[4]

[2] *Statement on the Immigration Bill 1971* (British Council of Churches), p. 1.

[3] J. Gladwell, *Brown Face, Big Master* (IVP, 1969), pp. 53f.

[4] *Cf.* J. O. Buswell, 'Sambo and Jim Crow', in *The Other Side*, vol. 8, no. 1, 1972.

Even our use of language may betray a legacy of prejudice. When Lord Hailsham (then Mr Quintin Hogg) said, 'I would rather be a black man with a white heart, than a white man with a black heart,'[5] he was intending to pay non-white immigrants a compliment, but his use of the words 'white' and 'black' to describe a man's disposition (his 'heart') shows how carelessly we can use colour terms to express values. English idiom abounds in expressions which equate 'black' with 'bad' or 'inferior'. I may put a relative in my 'black books', give him a 'black look' and treat him as the 'black sheep' of the family. Even gospel talks are not immune from criticism on this score. Some children's evangelists use the 'wordless book', with its different coloured pages, as a useful visual aid for communicating the gospel – but the 'sin' page is always coloured black. It is interesting to notice that the Bible occasionally describes sin as red (e.g. Is. 1: 18), but never as black.

The people of Bible times knew all about racial friction, but colour prejudice was apparently not much of a problem to them. The only representatives of the black races we meet in Scripture are the Ethiopians, and they seem to have been accepted on exactly the same terms as anyone else. Jeremiah, for example, refers to the Ethiopians' colour explicitly (13: 23), but without any derogatory overtones. He also tells the story of one outstanding black man, Ebed-melech, who held down an important job on King Zedekiah's staff in Jerusalem, and who later was promised special deliverance as a reward for his courage and ingenuity in rescuing the prophet (chs. 38 f.). The New Testament does not recognize any colour-bar either. Luke allows no hint of awkwardness or embarrassment to creep into his record of Philip's meeting with the Ethiopian eunuch. This dark-skinned man had apparently been worshipping freely in Jerusalem along with everybody else, and his carriage had no 'blacks only' notice on it to deter the olive-skinned Philip from accepting his invitation to jump up and explain the Scriptures (Acts 8: 26 ff.).

[5] Quoted by D. Bronnert, *Race*, p. 4.

115

Jesus himself, of course, did not have the pink-skinned, blue-eyed look that so many western artists mistakenly give him. Nor was he as black as a Negro. The Son of God would no doubt have been banned from a whites-only church in South Africa. He might also have been ejected from a Black Power convention in Harlem.

2. The redemption of man

God's concern for the redemption of mankind reaches beyond all man-made racial barriers, according to the Bible. His love extends to the whole world of men (Jn. 3: 16). He desires all men to be saved from the consequences of sin (1 Tim. 2: 4), through Christ's all-embracing death on the cross (2 Cor. 5: 19).

The focus for racial bitterness in New Testament times was the conflict between Jew and Gentile, and Jesus earned himself the hatred of many through his generous treatment of non-Jews such as the Syro-Phoenician woman from Tyre (Mk. 7: 24 ff.). In particular, the way he commended a Roman centurion (Mt. 8: 5 ff.) must have drawn the same gasps of astonishment from his hearers as would greet a member of the Ku Klux Klan today if he were overheard extolling the virtues of a negro houseboy. And Jesus achieved the reconciliation he lived and preached when he died on the cross. 'He is our peace,' the Jewish Paul reminds his Gentile readers at Ephesus, 'who has made us both one, and has broken down the dividing wall of hostility.' Jesus went to the cross, according to Paul, not only to repair the sin-breach between God and the individual Jew and Gentile. He died to 'reconcile . . . *both* to God in one body through the cross, thereby bringing the hostility to an end' (Eph. 2: 14, 16).

As a result of Christ's reconciling death, therefore, all divisive racial partitions between Christians are smashed. 'There is neither Jew nor Greek,' Paul writes; 'for you are all one in Christ Jesus' (Gal. 3: 28). 'Here there cannot be Greek and Jew, circumcised and uncircumcised, barbarian,

Scythian, slave, free man, but Christ is all, and in all' (Col. 3: 11).

After this, it comes as no surprise to discover from the last book of the Bible that there is no racial segregation in heaven. The congregation standing before the throne and before the Lamb in John's vision comes 'from every nation, from all tribes and peoples and tongues' (Rev. 7: 9).

Langston Hughes' attractive negro character, Jesse B. Semple, found that the way into heaven was not quite so accessible for a black man as these words appear to suggest. Waiting for him at the gate, beside St Peter, he found a white Southern Governor who insisted that he enter heaven by the back 'Coloured Entrance'. When Jesse protested, 'Anyway, Peter, is not my sins washed whiter than snow? Am I not white now inside and out?', the Governor butted in: 'You have to bathe in the River of Life to be washed whiter than snow. The River of Life is in heaven. You are not inside yet, Semple. Therefore, you are still black. White is right, black get back! You are not coming in the front entrance.'[6]

With his own racist background in mind, Peter would no doubt have some fellow-feeling for the race-conscious governor, but as a disciple of Jesus Christ he would have had to correct him on his theology. Here on earth, Christians are expected to anticipate the future by the way they live now. Their oneness in Christ is not to be simply a mystical unity forging a spiritual link between segregated congregations, but a living bond to be expressed in very practical ways (by eating together, for example, and by sitting together in church – Gal. 2: 14; cf. Jas. 2: 1–7).

3. The influence of sin
As Stafford-Clark, the psychologist, has wisely put it: 'No one is born prejudiced against others, but everyone is born prejudiced in favour of himself.'[7] And it is only a short

---

[6] L. Hughes, *Semple's Uncle Sam* (Hill and Wang, 1968), pp. 95f.

[7] Quoted in *Christians, Community and Race* (BCC).

step from prejudice in favour of oneself to prejudice in favour of the social unit to which one belongs. The group may be the family (how parents used to fight to get their children through the 11 + !) or the nation (in which case prejudice is upgraded to patriotism); it may involve defending one's colour, or taking pride in one's race. Most racial discord today does not reflect an implacable hatred for people of another group. It has its roots in pride, and even more frequently in fear, which is the obverse of pride. The Afrikaner is afraid of losing control of his country's mineral and industrial wealth. The British suburban dweller fears for the value of his property if his street is invaded by coloured families. And the prejudice which expresses these fears breeds hostility and discrimination, if it is left unchecked.

Prejudice in favour of oneself is, according to the Bible, the antithesis of Christian love, and must therefore clearly be labelled as sin. The Bible encourages group loyalty, but it condemns self-seeking, and one of the major criticisms of any apartheid policy is that by segregating racial communities it provides a cosy nest in which the eggs of prejudice can hatch out without disturbance. Discrimination may not be the declared aim of apartheid, but self-prejudiced human nature will always ensure that the segregators are treated more fairly than the segregated. As David Bronnert tersely comments, equality under apartheid tends to be of the 50/50 horse-and-rabbit-meat sandwich variety, when the recipe is one rabbit to one horse.[8] In Rhodesia, half the land is occupied by the white population and half by the black, which sounds a perfectly fair arrangement – until the statistics reveal that there are four million black people to 200,000 whites living in the country. In South Africa, the nine self-governing Bantustans, with their impressive libraries, churches, community halls and sports facilities, occupy just 13 per cent of the available land-space. The rest (which includes all the cities, ports and industrial

[8] D. Bronnert, 'Race Relations', in *Christian Graduate*, March 1970, p. 5.

118

complexes) is allocated to the 33 per cent of the population whose skin colour qualifies them to live in the 'white homeland'. The non-white residential zones are so far away from places of employment that Bantu workers have to leave home for months at a time in order to get regular work; a factor which (despite the help of the 'extended family') puts enormous strains on marriage and family life.

In the deadly serious business of self-protection, the stronger partner (who may be in a numerical minority) usually wins. But not always. In March 1973, *The Times* reported that a white man who accidentally stabbed himself with a bread knife bled to death because the only ambulance available to take him to hospital was reserved for coloureds. In her frustration and grief his widow vowed to write to the Prime Minister and his wife to tell them how apartheid had killed her husband and destroyed her life. 'I never dreamed apartheid was so cruel,' she told the reporter.[9] A policy of segregation leaves little room for neighbour-love, despite all the outward signs of social concern.

Successive attempts in Britain to formulate a water-tight immigration law have shown just how resilient racial prejudice can be. An Act of 1965 forbade the practice of racial discrimination in public places, and set up the Race Relations Board to deal with complaints, but the PEP report of 1967 still disclosed evidence of discrimination 'varying in extent from the massive to the substantial'.[1] The government responded with the Race Relations Act of 1968, which covered homes and jobs as well as the provision of goods and services. Nevertheless, when Sir Geoffrey Wilson took up his post as chairman of the Race Relations Board in 1971, he expressed his 'outrage' at the amount of racial discrimination still existing in the areas of housing and employment.[2] At about the same time, the results of a survey among managing directors showed that half of those asked did not sub-

[9] Report by Stanley Clys, *The Times*, 24 March 1973.
[1] *Racial Discrimination* (Political and Economic Planning).
[2] *The Times*, 2 November 1971.

scribe to the view that racial discrimination is a wrong principle.[3]

Contemporary history proves that sin is a hardy perennial, and the New Testament amply demonstrates how difficult it is to eradicate racial prejudice, without giving it an ideal habitat in which to grow and breed. Peter's example is perhaps the most telling one. Brought up as a strict racist, Peter the Jew would have no dealings with Gentiles – until, that is, the Holy Spirit taught him by a vision and a visit that there are no racial partitions in God's kingdom (Acts 10: 28). Peter won a famous victory over ingrained prejudice that day, or so it must have seemed at the time. But it was not long afterwards that he succumbed to the old temptations all over again, and earned Paul's criticism by excusing himself from Gentile hospitality while a strict Jewish delegation was in town (Gal. 2: 11 ff.).

If the pressures of prejudice proved too much for a disciple of Peter's calibre, what hope, we may ask, is there for us? Would it not be better to cut our losses, as the segregationists suggest, and avoid inevitable friction by separating the antagonists? Paul's stinging rebuke to Peter gives us the answer. The gospel demands that prejudice must be countered by Christian love. It is a pseudo-gospel, a denial of the reconciling power of Jesus, which advocates segregation as the final cure for racial hostility.

To sum up, the Bible lays two major responsibilities on every Christian.

1. To fight discrimination and prejudice
In spite of the vast changes in social conditions today, the main thrust of God's command to his people in Old Testament times is still relevant: 'the stranger who sojourns with you shall be to you as the native among you, and you shall love him as yourself' (Lv. 19: 34). The God of the Bible is passionately concerned for social justice. Whenever,

[3] *The Times*, 5 November 1971.

therefore, one person is treated less favourably than another on grounds of colour, race or national origin (which is how the Race Relations Act of 1968 defines discrimination), the Christian must protest in God's name.

Sometimes, the law of the land can be invoked to gain justice for the oppressed. But the law, however useful a weapon it may prove in the fight against discrimination, is relatively powerless against prejudice. Prejudice is an attitude of mind, and as such is beyond the reach of legislation. The law can deal effectively only with actions and words. It may influence ideas and opinions indirectly, but it cannot control them. A restaurant proprietor, for example, may be compelled by law to take down the 'No Coloureds' notice from his window, because that is discrimination. But no Act of Parliament can ever eradicate the racial prejudice that continues to simmer in his mind and heart.

Significantly, it was at the level of heart and mind that Jesus aimed his most demanding instructions, and the Christian is bound to follow the Master's example. Selfishness, jealousy and fear must be challenged and exposed wherever they appear. In order to unravel mixed motives, and combat rumour and misinterpretation, one of the Christian's first duties will no doubt be to 'do a Wilberforce' and create an informed public opinion on matters of race and colour. Is it generally known, for example, that emigrants from Britain have outnumbered immigrants for at least the last decade? Or that the immigrant community costs the tax-payer over 15 per cent less, per head, than the native white population?[4] And in addition to challenging popularly held misconceptions at home, Christians are particularly well placed, through their missionary knowledge of conditions in developing countries overseas, to provide more information which may help to silence the scaremongers.

It is, of course, a matter of hot dispute whether disciples

[4] Evidence from *Facts and Figures*, published by the British Council of Churches Community and Race Relations Unit and the Institute of Race Relations.

of Jesus should ever use economic or political force to further the advance of social justice. Should investors be encouraged to sell their shares in South African companies, in the hope that the sponsors of apartheid will be brought to their knees economically? Is it more important to preserve order and stability in a country like South Africa than to promote freedom and moral reform through revolution? These are urgent issues in their own right, and it would take another chapter to debate the cases for and against, for example, the World Council of Churches' special fund for freedom fighters. But however wide the disagreement about legitimate means, all Christians should be united in their basic determination to combat racial discrimination and prejudice. And whatever else this may entail, it will certainly call for courage to face opposition and unpopularity, and plain speaking to cut through the protective verbiage of vested interests.

2. To work for integration

'Integration' is a word that can be used in several different ways. A spoonful of sugar, for example, may be successfully 'integrated' in a cup of coffee, with the result that it loses its separate identity altogether. There are some who would like to see coloured immigrants integrated into the British community in this drastic way – abandoning their native dress, language and customs, and if possible painting themselves an acceptable shade of pink to disguise their distinctiveness. But to ask this of any immigrant is to rob him of personal identity, which is a basic human right. It also robs the community at large of the cultural richness newcomers should be able to contribute to it. A brick wall provides a better illustration of the kind of unity Christians should be striving to achieve. In a wall, each brick keeps its separate identity, while being firmly bonded to the rest. It was this sort of integration that Roy Jenkins had in mind when he defined his aim for immigrants as 'not a flattening process of assimilation, but as equal opportunity, accompanied by cultural diversity, in an atmosphere of mutual tolerance'.[5]

Love demands that Christians should strive to unite and reconcile those who would otherwise live at daggers drawn. In practical terms (and biblical love is practical, not sentimental), this may involve fostering children, taking time to learn about a strange culture, or teaching English in Asian homes, as well as publishing manifestos and lobbying local councillors. It is only when biblical ideals are lived out that the world sits up and takes notice. 'Are Christians interested?' asks David Bronnert in his booklet on *Race*. 'Do they care? If not, they will make it difficult for others to believe the gospel, for the claim that God reconciles men to each other and makes them loving caring people needs to be seen as well as believed.'[6]

The path will not be a smooth one, as any social worker can testify. Those who work for integration in multi-racial areas are up against the prejudice of the immigrant who prefers to retreat into a ghetto rather than learn a new language or change customs which his neighbours find offensive, as well as the selfishness of the established resident who resents the intrusion of newcomers. Sometimes feelings may run so high that segregation seems the only practical solution for the time being. It may be necessary, for example, to house coloured families in such a way that their exposure to discrimination will be minimized. But if this means segregating them, it must be seen as a temporary expedient, not a final solution. The end in view, the Christian has to insist, is nothing less than full integration – especially in the church, where any kind of spiritual apartheid is ruled out altogether by New Testament teaching.

Questions for discussion

1. How would you answer the specific points raised by 'A case for apartheid' on pp. 104–111?

[5] Quoted in *Christians, Community and Race*.
[6] D. Bronnert, *Race*, p. 20.

2. Pinpoint the differences between discrimination and prejudice. From the Christian point of view, how may both be dealt with most effectively?

3. What practical steps could be taken to promote integration in your neighbourhood?

For further reading

D. Bronnert, *Race* (Falcon, 1973)

T. B. Maston, *Segregation and Desegregation* (Macmillan, 1959)

C. S. Hill, *Immigration and Integration* (Pergamon, 1970)

Free to do Right

DAVID FIELD

This short book grapples with many of the
moral problems facing young people today.
As the author points out in his preface,
'doing the right thing is not easy. Even
finding out what it is can sometimes be
difficult.' His chief aim has therefore been to
draw out the main guide-lines provided by
the Bible for those seeking their moral
bearings, but at every stage he has tried to
'earth' the argument by direct reference to the
moral issues in today's headlines.

112 pages

An IVP Pocketbook.

Principles of Conduct

JOHN MURRAY

Are we justified in speaking of norms, or standards, in the behaviour sanctioned by the Bible? And, if there are norms, how are they derived? Is there one coherent and consistent ethic set out in the Bible, or does the New Testament contradict the Old?

In these studies John Murray, formerly Professor of Systematic Theology in Westminster Theological Seminary, Philadelphia, discusses such topics as marriage, the ordinance of labour, the sanctity of life, law and grace. He aims to show the basic unity and continuity of the biblical ethic.

272 pages

Inter-Varsity Press.

Studies in the Sermon on the Mount

D. MARTYN LLOYD-JONES

The Sermon on the Mount (Matthew 5–7) is one of the best-known passages in the Bible, but it is also one of the most frequently misunderstood and misapplied. Here Dr Martyn Lloyd-Jones, formerly Minister of Westminster Chapel, London, gives a fresh insight into the Sermon as he seeks to explain and apply Christ's teaching.

Volume 1 (320 pages) contains a general introduction to the passage, followed by detailed exposition of Matthew 5.
Volume 2 (338 pages) continues with the exposition of chapters 6 and 7.

Inter-Varsity Press.